# THE END OF LOVE

Tamara Tenenbaum

# THE END
# OF LOVE

*Translated from the Spanish
by Carolina Parodi*

Europa
*editions*

Europa Editions
27 Union Square West, Suite 302
New York NY 10003
www.europaeditions.com
info@europaeditions.com

Translation by Carolina Parodi
Original title: *El fin del amor*
Translation copyright © 2024 by Europa Editions

Library of Congress Cataloging in Publication Data is available
ISBN 979-8-88966-010-1

Tenenbaum, Tamara
The End of Love

Cover design by Ginevra Rapisardi

Prepress by Grafica Punto Print—Rome

Printed in the USA

# CONTENTS

*Your love does not travel first class.*
—CELESTE CARBALLO

# THE END
# OF LOVE

There's a neighborhood in Brooklyn that feels like a slice of Israel—to those who have never been. The street signs are written in a language that resembles Hebrew but is in fact Yiddish, which uses the same alphabet. The protagonists of the billboards on the streets are bearded men in hats. The women you see, as well as being covered almost from head to toe, all wear the same, the exact same stockings in white, gray, or black. Wearing skin-colored stockings is forbidden; there are signs throughout the neighborhood that state this. I assume that to save themselves the trouble of having to decide whether the stockings resemble the color of their legs, women only buy their stockings from the local store, which sells only those authorized. This is why they all wear the same ones. "Look," my mother told me the first time we entered the neighborhood and crossed paths with some of its inhabitants. "The women walk behind the men. There aren't many people from this Orthodox sect left in Argentina." She gestured at them, trying and failing not to point too much.

My mother, my sisters, and I grew up in a Jewish Orthodox community known as Modern Orthodox. There are many of us in the streets of Buenos Aires: girls who keep their heads covered but wear denim skirts, men who don't wear big hats or have "curly sidelocks" but do have a beard and wear a kippah. I was born in 1989 in Once and lived there until I was twenty-three, when I moved in with a friend. In metaphysical terms, I was fortunate to be able to leave early, though in another sense, one never truly leaves. I'm surprised when I see Hasidic Jewish men in New York walking in front of the women they're with, but not that surprised. My mother, who is a doctor and continues to work in the neighborhood, has many patients like that, or more or less like that. Almost all my middle school friends are married and have a second, third, or fourth child on the way. The same goes for my younger sisters' schoolfriends.

In the documentary *One of Us*, two men and a woman my age share how difficult it was to leave the Hasidic community they belonged to, the same one I witnessed in New York. I got off lightly, but when I watched this Netflix documentary, I particularly identified with two recurring themes in the stories, which are, in reality, the same theme. The first is the absolute ignorance of everything that is happening in the "real world." Sometimes it's hard to explain that, although you live there—in a large city among everyone, among all kinds of people, even if you have a TV or internet (I did but the people from the documentary didn't)—, it's as if you lived on a different planet. Until the age of twelve, I didn't know what ham looked like, let alone tasted like. I didn't know if it resembled a pig or a steak, or what people ate it with. I certainly never suspected it would look like cold cuts, as Jewish people barely have any except pastrami, so it wasn't a concept I could easily grasp. House cleaners are called shiksa—a derogatory term that does not mean "black" or "slave," but "not Jewish"—and are the only non-Jewish girls an Orthodox Jew knows. One night, my mother noticed I was dying to break Shabbat and play at being normal, so she asked the girl who cleaned our house if she would invite me to her movie night, which she had planned with two of her girlfriends (when I recall this story, I realize my childhood wasn't as racist and classist as I thought). I think we watched an Adam Sandler movie at the cinema, and I'm certain that we ate popcorn, because I had never had popcorn before. I was fascinated by how fearless Juana and her friends were: the way they moved, the way they ate and talked, the way they got on the bus and spoke to this or that man.

Although the film was the least interesting detail that night, the second theme that is repeated throughout the documentary and that also runs through my life, is the importance of culture in the widest imaginable sense of the word. This means everything from soap operas or a book by Mario Vargas Llosa I found on the bookshelf in the sitting room, to the entry of sexuality in the *Encyclopaedia Britannica*. Everything that refers to the world beyond your home and your neighborhood you devour with passion: everything that talks, above all, about sex, but also about friendship, money, work, homes, clothes, and food. One of the men in the documentary claims that finding Wikipedia was one of the best moments of his life. I was a little older than him when Wikipedia became popular in Argentina, but I perfectly understood the dizziness associated with the feeling that a secret window is suddenly being opened, a secret window showing everything everyone else is talking about, a window from which you can eavesdrop on a conversation you don't understand without anyone watching you, without them finding out that you don't know what *morcillas* are or what a thong is.

I was fortunate, firstly, because my community was not as closed-minded as those seen in *One of Us*. At school, we followed the official curriculum (though it didn't include sexual education) and I was allowed to watch television and go to the movies, as were most of my friends. At home, education and culture were important, an Ashkenazi tradition I guess. Though my mother was never a great follower of art, she felt it was important to take us to museums and encourage us to develop reading habits, without controlling too much what we were reading. In a sense, this was a double-edged sword. Some of my peers could clearly see that what we found in fiction was exotic in comparison with their lives. "That's not for us," one of my sister's friends used to say, referring to the lives of the girls in popular soap operas, as if it were obvious and without explaining why. Some of us were seduced by that parallel universe that seemed to be so close—happening in the neighborhoods we frequented, outside shopping malls we visited—yet so far away. By complete coincidence, I became one of them. My father passed away when I was five years old. I was the eldest and, as my sisters and I were growing up, my mother began allowing some rule-bending at home while keeping up appearances in the neighborhood of Once. After a few years, we also gave that up. I suppose that having to follow so many rules was far from convenient while juggling with the demands of three little girls at home. I don't know how they would have entertained us without turning the television on during Shabbat, when my mom would be doing shifts at the emergency room every Saturday. No one wanted to stop us from doing things any more than was absolutely necessary. I didn't realize this at the time, but my mom's first few years of being a widow were difficult emotionally and financially. By the time I was able to understand, things were better in both senses, and we had one foot in and one out of our religion.

Though we were gradually distancing ourselves from the community, it was still a ground-breaking moment when I told mother that I wanted to go to "a good school," those that prepare you to go to university. She accepted. Luck was on my side again. I didn't have to fight anyone to the death or run away from home to be able to build a new life and become a different person. I was the first one to try ham, to have non-Jewish friends, and to buy a sleeveless top to wear out in the streets without another layer. Though not everything was as easy. My mom cried when I told her I wanted to go to an end-of-year dance at Guadalupe school, where one of my friends from the induction course to state high school was finishing middle school. "I understand you're going to a secular school, but dancing cumbia with the boys from church?" It was like a scene from *My Yiddishe Momme* with the added melodrama of an Italian movie. I did not go to that dance, and it was not as tragic as it seemed back then.

When I arrived at the new school, I felt like I'd walked into an abyss. I obviously didn't know any of the rules. I'd accumulated a certain amount of knowledge, or so I believed, but it was entirely based on fiction, and I began doubting how useful it would be when applied to the real world. How old should you say you were when you first kissed someone on the lips? What kind of interaction should you have with boys in your daily life? Do you always peck boys in the cheek when saying hello or only if you know them already? Should you wear miniskirts every day or consciously mix it up? Is losing your virginity before marriage as common as it is in films? These are questions I would constantly ask myself, explicitly, every time I was part of a conversation or at one of my new girlfriend's birthday parties, or simply when I was alone at home with spare time to think through and organize these ideas. I should clarify, in case it isn't obvious, that in the world where I came from (come from), there is a single answer to all these questions. Orthodox Jews have clear rules for everything—food, clothes, the way we behave around the opposite sex, even rules surrounding menstruation. Most of them are written down somewhere in the Torah or the Talmud and, if there was ever any doubt about any of them, the Rabbi would offer an example as an answer. In the world I was becoming a part of, the urban middle class of the twenty-first century, there were not any sacred scriptures, and so I began to think that maybe there weren't many rules, either.

The question regarding human relationships was the one I found the most complicated. I was a good student largely because of the appetite for knowledge and curiosity I felt after having lived a reclusive life, which also nurtured a love for reading. But there weren't any books that explained everything I didn't understand, nor were there any people I could go to for answers. I would have never dared ask, plus these are the kind of things people are not even aware they know. So I decided to watch and listen, to try to make up principles and meanings out of the stories that others would tell me, out of what people said about their parents' relationships or about the boys they liked. To figure out if saying hello to a boy with a kiss on the cheek actually was an erotic gesture (as it was for me, given that in my neighborhood this was forbidden) or if it was a simple routine that had lost all affective meaning. To figure out whether other girls got goosebumps when a boy put their arms around them for a photo. To figure out if they knew whether their older sisters were sexually active or if their aunts were being unfaithful.

This led me to a second discovery: it's not that there weren't any rules. People couldn't simply do whatever they pleased. The rules were just less strict and more invisible; more confusing, yet still there. There were certain behaviors that would catalogue you as a whore, others as a fool, others as ridiculous, or crazy. My third discovery was that nobody else, and in particular, none of the other girls, were as clear on these rules as I had thought. They were all scared of doing things wrong. They were all as eager as I was to understand the rules governing their bodies. They were ahead of me in certain topics, but from the kiss on the cheek to spin the bottle, it was an even playing field and we were all equally lost and tormented. That didn't change with the years. When you finally solved the kissing dilemma, you had to worry about sex. Once you understood boyfriends, you had to think about children. The finish line was continuously being moved forward. None of my girlfriends would claim today to understand anything about love or sex, let alone what happens around and in-between them. The wisest of them have already lost hope of ever understanding it.

This book comes from this story, my compulsion for listening, reading, investigating, thinking about human bonds. At university I read philosophy because I like to systematize what I learn, hear, read, what I am told, and what happens to me—particularly when it relates to issues that resist being organized into systems. I know that once you walk beyond the borders of Once, there are no manuals on how to menstruate or how to have sex and I don't believe they will ever exist. Freedom will always be this distressing, and I'd bet against anyone who challenges that notion. I remember life on that side of Córdoba Avenue all too well, and the alternative, freedom, is better. Yet, I believe such matters often get a bad press. Literature about them is considered to be cheap self-help rather than social criticism, nonsense that nobody cares about—or at least not anybody who matters. These are believed to be bourgeois problems, as if people with fewer resources did not have desires, did not have sex, did not love, did not also feel lonely. As if thinking too much about these topics were an obsessive and unhealthy habit. For those of us who do not know how to "let go," I believe that thinking and writing about these issues is a way of coming together.

My mother still lives and works in Once. I don't think there's anyone left who is religious in my family—we don't go to the synagogue, though we do get together for the festivities like any other non-practicing Jewish family. Strangers are very intrigued by our meals. When we celebrate Passover and Rosh Hashanah, we do the full version, including all the traditions that most people aren't familiar with. It's like the "behind the scenes" side in the DVDs we used to buy that included alternative endings and interviews with the cast.

I have now had over fifteen years of immersion in the Western world. I went to a state university, read philosophy, and ended up working as a journalist. These are not easy times for my trade but I usually have work so I can't complain. I teach at the university I attended and, as the age gap between my students and I grows, I increasingly feel that this space is necessary, even vital. I left home at the same age as my non-Jewish friends, I had sex and took drugs like any other of my school friends, less than some and more than others. I no longer wake up fearing that one day I will be allocated a husband and sent back to Once, a recurrent nightmare I had until I was twenty years old. I still find things I don't quite understand about life in the secular world every day and I doubt that will ever change, but I recognize that having experienced life on the other side has its advantages. Although I didn't enter a world free of rules, I can appreciate the huge privileges and freedom I enjoy. When my friends from university complain that they are underpaid and that, at the age of eighteen, they thought that by the time they were thirty they would be in a different position, I laugh. In my case, being able to choose to live alone, be financially independent, and be with whoever I want to be whenever I want makes me extremely fortunate. These are things I'm grateful for every day, things I ardently hope will soon be the reality of all the women in the world.

I am writing with awareness of my situation as a Latin American woman and daughter of a single mother, but also of my privilege as part of the middle class of Buenos Aires and of the limitations set by my own heterosexual experience. This book is not a study of social science. This presumes, of course, certain limitations when it comes to the intention of thinking outside of my own self. I do, however, insert myself with modesty and feminist ambition in a long and rich tradition of female writers who, through their personal history (from Virginia Woolf to Laurie Penny, from Virginie Despentes to Remedios Zafra) contributed to starting conversations that went way beyond themselves. This does not guarantee anything, but a precedent already exists.

A necessary disclaimer: this book fundamentally explores the specifics of the heterosexual bond. I believe that queer relationships have their own history, their own conversations, and their own theoretical issues. Changing pronouns to talk about "all the kinds of relationships" is not enough. I often refer to queer bibliography and concepts, and I also draw upon lessons from the LGBTQI+ community that come from a history of living outside of the norm. I guess a lot of what I write can also be applied to relationships of every kind, but I believe that there is something specific about heterosexuality, which is its relationship with the norm and with a specific type (not biological, but social and historical) of asymmetry. This asymmetry has an effect that is probably not experienced in the same way in other types of relationships, and I do not expect that what I say in this book lends itself to a generalization to be applied to all those other types of relationships.

The other limitation I must apologize for, though it concerns all philosophical thought, is that, inevitably, throughout books like these one can find words and phrases such as "women," "men," "girls from my generation," and other examples and formulations of the kind. Generalizations are a problem, but they are necessary if we want to transcend individuality and talk about what we have in common with other people of the same gender, origins, age, and social class. I never presume that what I say applies to all the cases, from the first to the last, nor am I, more importantly, at any point throughout this book speaking of unmodifiable destinies, biological determinants, or timeless entelechies. I use the word "woman" (and "man") as Marxist feminist Silvia Federici explains it in her book *Caliban and the Witch*[1]—as a cultural, but also economical, resource. More specifically, I use the terms as historical categories that signal social position rather than an immutable identity or one tied to any kind of biological circumstance.

I wanted to use my own history as a starting point because,

though it might seem specific to me, it could in fact be anyone's story. We all arrive as foreigners in the world of desire and go through a never-ending process of learning its language. This book is not a dictionary or a behavioral manual like those your mothers or grandmothers gave you, but it can perhaps become a travel journal, or at least I hope that it will.

# CHAPTER 1
## THE FEMALE VERSION OF JAMES DEAN

The girls from the secular world I met at school followed the religion of love. Whether their origins were Christian, Jewish, or even Buddhist on one occasion, none of them had been taught to follow as many arbitrary rules as I had been growing up in the Orthodox Jewish community. They had grown up with what I interpreted as total freedom, which never ceased to amaze me. If they wanted to stop eating broccoli, they did; if they didn't want to join the Sunday family outing, they didn't join (most of them didn't even have "Sunday family plans"); if they didn't want their younger sisters to tag along with them on Friday nights, they wouldn't take them. They had their own money. It was a question of individuality rather than financial stability. They would be given monthly allowances like in movies, and they spent it on things their parents didn't know about. I was given what I asked for, but I had to ask for it. Their parents wouldn't open the bathroom door while they were in the shower, and their sisters wouldn't take your clothes without asking first. Anyone who knows how a Jewish household works knows that privacy is a principle we don't have—according to my mother, for example, "we share clothes." When someone asked me what I wanted to do when I finished school, I couldn't think of an answer other than "go to university" (and I felt very lucky to not have to say "get married, have twelve kids and raise them following the Torah."). Other girls talked about backpacking trips abroad, about learning how to play the guitar, of taking time off to figure things out.

No one had ever told me that dedicating time to pleasure or to not doing anything was allowed, that life wasn't a boardgame in which we always had to be moving one space forward. Because of all of this, it took me years to understand that these girls weren't the very image of freedom and prosperity either, and that they had also inherited a system of beliefs based on long-held traditions that preceded them. It simply worked in a different way.

The girls from my high school were brilliant. I watched them grow and become political scientists, engineers, actors, and doctors. When they thought no one was watching them they were witty, fun, and could talk about anything. Despite this, a large amount of our time was spent on boyfriends: we spoke more about boys than politics, books, clothes, and television. We didn't compare ourselves like boys did by our sporting aptitude or how much we knew about 70s rock bands. The only questions we asked were: Do you have a boyfriend, have you ever had a boyfriend, and how old were you when you had your first boyfriend? Those of us who hadn't had one, lied. I never confirmed it, but I don't think I was the only one.

Little by little, I also converted to the religion of love, but at the start, this new way of seeing the world filled me with bewilderment, though it was very difficult to explain why. It's not that I was born Simone de Beauvoir, but in Orthodox Judaism, romantic relationships as an entity independent from the family did not exist. When as feminists, we talk about the need to deconstruct[1] "romantic love" and "a traditional family," we often believe them to be the same thing, but the history of these two institutions is more complex than that. Investigating this history helped me understand not only my own personal journey, but also the reason why women in the twenty-first century find it a lot more complicated to break free from the first than the second one.

What today we consider as a romantic relationship or

romantic love (the idea that a relationship should be based solely on a mutual and free attraction between two people who are perfect for each other, the most important person in each other's world—or at least excepting their children) is a very young ideal in comparison to its parent, grandparent or even great-grandparent institution: marriage. Of course, these two social constructs are intimately related, and one could not have come into being without the other; however, what we currently view as the definitive characteristic of a couple, love between two people, was for centuries a bonus of marriage, something that was not part of its core definition.

In her book *Marriage, a History: How Love Conquered Marriage*,[2] Stephanie Coontz retraces the beginnings of the institution of marriage in all different civilizations throughout the ages. There is a connecting thread, and perhaps even an objective, throughout this trajectory: to demonstrate at which point the idea of marrying "for love" becomes a historical novelty. As Coontz explains in the first chapter, love is not, as we often understand, a new concept essentially. In many societies that are physically and temporarily far removed from ours, love is thought of in a similar way; however, the idea that such a changing and capricious feeling is a good reason to marry, or *the* reason to marry, was ridiculous for members of those societies.

For a long time, marriage was not thought of as the union between two people, but rather as the union between two families that would form a profitable and mutually beneficial association. The path that culminates in the contemporary romantic relationship was not linear. Coontz explains that as humans evolved into sedentary beings and accumulated an increasing amount of productive surplus, financial disparities between families accentuated. Young people (both women and men) were no longer free to choose their partners in the same way generations that preceded sedentarism had. This power then fell into the hands of the figureheads who decided which marriage was most convenient for the collective. Women were considered exchangeable goods or olive branches offered to formalize a commercial alliance or to decrease animosity with another family. What better way to achieve this than through our daughters?

This worked for many different civilizations up until less than two-hundred years ago and it still works in some places.[3] Coontz cites some rather bizarre cases to illustrate how the union between two individuals was far less important than the union between families: in China and Sudan, for example, if two families wanted to form an alliance but only one of them had single, living children of an appropriate age, they could arrange a marriage between a young person and a spirit or a ghost. In the beginning of the twentieth century, young women who wanted to please their families but did not want to live with a man, sought these ghost marriages as most parents would not allow for more than one of their daughters to remain single. Evidently, progeny was not the main objective of marriage. Children, at least for these families, were less important than brothers-in-law. There was such a shortage of "ghosts" that when a young man passed away, he became a coveted soul for all the single women aware of the normative loophole who wanted to continue to live alone and in peace.

Except for the "detail" of children, which for Orthodox Jews are very important, life in Once is similar. If a family objects to a marriage (not all religious marriages are one-hundred percent arranged—in the more modern sectors of Orthodox communities especially, it is common to see young people meet in shared spaces and families limiting themselves to authorizing the union), it isn't because they have a problem with the boy or the girl, whose qualities are somewhat irrelevant. The true parameter for measuring desirability or a lack of it in a marriage is the family of origin of each interested party. In fact, the contrary is relatively common, a typical tale of a wretched princess:

parents forcing a girl to marry an unattractive candidate of little intelligence and kindness, merely because he comes from a good family. It's difficult to explain, but this is not done out of spite. Orthodox Jews, like all societies with traditional or pre-modern values, do not believe in the idea of individualism, which is one of the conceptual pillars of modern romantic love.[4] If we didn't believe each person to be unique, special, and irreplaceable, falling in love with someone in particular would not make sense. In this way, the unspoken assumption in Once is that even when there are negative rumors about the prospective betrothed, if he comes from a good family, he must be a good person deep down. At the very least, in objective terms, marrying him is still a good idea. Subjective terms do not exist in a universe like this. A "good match" is a good match for anyone, not exclusively for one person.

In consequence, the upbringing of girls in the Orthodox Jewish community focuses on an idealization of family, the upbringing of children and housework, but not on their husbands, love, nor the romantic relationship. I don't recall having heard the word "partner" before starting high school, or anything about "relationship problems." No one in Once cares about this particular subtype of problem unless it escalates to a level that disrupts the rest of the family or the union *between* families. Although husband and wife must respect each other (asymmetrically, of course), no one expects them to be madly in love. It is perhaps not even beneficial that they are, for the good of familial peace and to achieve short, medium, and long-term equilibrium. No one needs a Prince Charming—a man who brings food to the table and cares about his children and his woman is enough.

This might sound unusual and unlikely in Western communities, but the West resembled what I am retelling here until not many years ago. A lot of grandmothers still talk of "a good match" or of "convenient marriages," only their daughters (our mothers) never listened. It is that small subversion that separated the world we live in from traditional societies. In the space between convenience and desire, between the familial and the personal, between marriage as a union of a collective and a couple as a relationship between two human beings, that which we call *romantic love* is born.

There is a certain continuity between the history of family as a concept and that of romantic love, but fundamentally, there is also a rupture. A rupture we have to think about to understand that freeing ourselves from one does not necessarily mean discarding the other. These are two different currents that incur different costs and pose different questions. Although the tale of romantic love is related to the development of Modernism and of contemporary currents of thought as well as to the ideas of individuality and freedom—its conceptual pillars—, the consolidation of these ways of thinking and of thinking of the self was neither a fast nor linear process. Consequently, neither was the arrival of romantic love.

The emblem of love in the West is the tragedy of Romeo and Juliet. It's interesting, but certainly no coincidence that the longevity of this story, first published in 1597, has by far surpassed any other Shakesperean tragedy as well as many love stories that followed. No other story has been adapted and re-adapted as many times as this one, and I am not only referring to explicit adaptations but also to the vast number of stories built upon the foundations of forbidden love, from *Titanic* to *Muñeca Brava*, the soap-opera starring Natalia Oreiro. The idea of love as an erotic force that is unleashed and more powerful than convention, tradition, and socio-economic structures is the pillar of a mass genre that is popular throughout the world, and particularly so in Latin America: melodrama.

Centennial women (those born after 1994 or 2000, depending on the definition) might find it somewhat outlandish, but millennials devoured classic soap-operas starring Thalía and others—just like our grandmothers devoured radio drama shows, movies, and Corín Tellado's novels—based on the same premise of a world with such rigid class and social divisions that only love can transgress. The person in love cuts themselves off from the social group they belong to, then love leads to their validation as an individual in their own right. This individual no longer represents the culture they come from, the family they were born into, nor the values they were taught; none of it matters. "Love above every social difference," as Rodrigo "el Potro" sings. The only thing that matters is that this person becomes an individual because another one has selected him or her for the most fundamental and freeing reason: love. No origins, no institution can transcend it. Romantic love is an effect of contemporary subjectivity. But not only that, we could say it also generates and reinforces subjectivity by questioning traditional institutions such as the family, clans, or a nation.

Love has the potential to make us more special and unique than our last names and origins. It unites but also divides—it separates us from who we thought we were or should become. The structure of Romeo and Juliet is the paradigm of modern love, and for that reason we cannot stop consuming it.[5] These stories reinforce the modern current of thought we are most preoccupied with preserving: that we are more than our race, our social class, our country, our families. That, although we are conditioned by all these intersections, we are more than the simple sum of them. There is something that makes us unique and irreplaceable which none of these categories covers and, if someone falls in love with us, they fall in love with that.

In every impossible love story, sons and daughters, teenagers, or young people like Romeo and Juliet are the ones who reject their families and values in order to experience love. Marriage can appear as something forced or forged (parents impose a "convenient" engagement over the one that the heart has chosen), but love is not, in these stories, a social imposition in the way forming a family is. On the contrary, it is a form of rebellion; it proposes transgressing respect for one's family (at least in the beginning). Little by little, through culture, love has conceptually cemented itself as a *specifically feminine form of rebellion*.

Though most modern heroes are men, the archetype of the woman who defies society to defend love is key in the construction of a particular kind of modern subjectivity that we keep questioning. In these stories, an evident and definitive characteristic of modern society is autonomy in the private sphere. In the neighborhood I was born in, having the Rabbi and your mother choose a boyfriend for you is not considered an invasion because, as I mentioned, getting married is not considered a "private" choice. The Rabbi can also suggest how many children a couple should have without anyone thinking that he is meddling. The idea of freedom does not play a key role, and it is also understood that decisions concerning getting married and starting a family are eminently financial and affect the couple in question, but also, and more importantly, their families.

Our modern heroines are not hugely practical, but that is part of their charm. They are not moved by money or other worldly motivations, and their love represents a protest against the tedious, prudent, and logical lives that bourgeois morality offers. They run barefoot with their hair down, neglecting what they are meant to be doing but are more like little girls than revolutionaries. Simone de Beauvoir studies the version of this archetype of the second half of the twentieth century in *Brigitte Bardot and the Lolita Syndrome*.[6] Having no worries, like a little girl who still does not need to preoccupy herself with the mundane matters of life, is not just another characteristic of the ideal "girl in love" of the sixties (inherited by the twenty-first century iteration, the Manic Pixie Dream Girl).[7] It is an essential part of the subjectivity surrounding the love story she comes to represent, opposing the idea of a "good wife" that mothers and behavioral manuals have imparted for centuries. These contemporary heroines do not have to contend with the moral punishment that tormented their ancestors centuries back (they generally don't die in the end, at least) but they do carry a fundamental tradition: the disdain for the material world and the commitment to a purely disinterested form of love.

True love, they say, we still say, is unrelated to money. But this is one of the most powerful illusions surrounding romantic love. By upholding that love is not concerned with rent or budgeting (in contrast with the image of a frigid housewife who counts every penny to be able to feed her family), what is dismissed is a truth known by the mothers of Once: that their daughters must marry not because they cannot be happy alone, but because someone must support them financially. Part of the deconstruction we must embark on regarding romantic love implies viewing this dissociation between love, money, and politics as a fictitious ideology in the most Marxist sense of the word: fiction that hides underlying power dynamics.

When feminist economists say "they say it is love, we say it is unwaged work," referring to housework that mainly falls on women (bored wives or passionate lovers), they are talking about this. The woman who sacrifices herself for love does not do it for no reason, she does it in the context of love supposedly being the only possible path toward a meaningful life and toward transcendence. Men can transcend through what they build, their productive work, their colonial power. A woman's best shot at being the protagonist of a great love story is being "the woman behind a great man," the one who looks after the children of the author of a wonderful story. A woman can do an infinite number of things, but if she does not have romantic love, socially she will be regarded as empty, as an incomplete individual. As if this was not enough, romantic love demands that, if that woman truly wishes to be loved, she cannot expect to be left with much. She must give her full self—her time, labor, her emotional disposition—because anything less than that is equivalent to nothing. But we do not expect a man to offer the same. It is not mandatory for him (nor expected, because a man who gives his all is not in love, he is under the thumb, emasculated) to give all of himself to prove his love. Those of us who have given ourselves to love imagined that by giving a man all our energy and time—relinquishing our friends and passions for a man who makes our hearts skip a beat—we've done something completely different to those women who married for convenience or obligation. We thought our concerns were of an immaterial, ethereal, intangible nature, when in fact, we were simply using different language to mask the material, financial and political exchanges at play. They disappear as if by magic.

On the other hand, the insurrection of the woman in love, just as the narrative of romantic love shows, is profoundly individualistic. Neither Juliet nor the princesses of fairy tales defy their parents. Adulterous women like Emma Bovary or Anna Karenina, or any soap-opera heroines do not aspire to change the rules, not even those who at some point understand the oppression exercised upon them. They rise above the hypocrisy of bourgeois morality through emotions and sacrifice, not through questioning or destruction. In fact, the only destruction we see in their stories is that of themselves. And this is perhaps the most intriguing point—romantic love does not even promise women eternal happiness. Many of these stories have happy endings, but a lot of them end badly for the female character. Yet in most of these stories, the woman still yearns to experience a passionate love affair, despite all consequences. It's as if these stories worked simultaneously as an incentive and a warning: the world will punish you for loving too much, don't doubt that for a second, but it's not worth living any other way. These stories end in punishment, death, losing one's voice or freedom or everything, so in that sense, we can't really say that we've been lied to. After all, the promise still works.

The unspoken question of the role of romantic love and its relationship with how we are supposed to be is everywhere. In magazines, radio shows, music, movies that our grandmothers and great-grandmothers consumed—from *Gone with the Wind* to the *boleros* of the trio Los Ponchos, and the pages of magazines like *Vosotras*, *Para Ti* and other women's magazines that circulated in Argentina from the thirties and reached peak popularity between the fifties and sixties. I spent many months reading and researching old women's magazines to be able to write answers as part of the agony aunt column in the newspaper *La Nación*. Finding them was no mean feat. They were historically considered so irrelevant that no archives are kept, except for *Para Ti* as it was produced by the publishing house Atlántida. I hunted for the rest of them at old bookshops or on e-commerce site Mercado Libre, and I could never find more than a couple. Tedious (and expensive) but worth it. From a feminist perspective, we can reclaim the importance of these spaces. It's true that they are full of stereotypes and preconceptions, but no more so than other publications that were considered more "serious" or "important" by the male gaze. Agony aunt columns, because of the type of relationship they establish between the author and the reader—letters would be signed with pseudonyms and sent using only first names—allowed journalists to discuss topics and anxieties that they perhaps would not have dared to publish had the submissions been signed. Far from the more scientific tone of the cover stories discussing family and marriage and quoting male psychologists and doctors who repeated heteronormative narratives relentlessly, one gets the impression that these columns gave women a space in which to speak (at least slightly) more openly.

Reading these agony aunt columns, I could see that the transformation of the discourse of love was slow, that there was a lot of back and forth. During times of change, two outlooks coexisted as the only possible models of happiness that were contradictory on surface level: a "good" marriage that is approved by the family and a wildly passionate love affair. After reading several issues published between the forties and late seventies, I began to discern some tendencies. From the mid-fifties onwards, the discourse surrounding romantic love appears mostly in fiction (short stories or novels mentioned in the magazines), while in the agony aunt columns or in letters from readers, the predominant topic was that of family harmony. "Nobody should have to tolerate constant meltdowns. Not only does this get old, it's also a waste of energy. Such is the case of your husband," answers Helena in the agony aunt column of *Vosotras* in the seventies. In the same issue, there is a fictionalized version of the history of Wallis Simpson, a divorced woman whose love made king Edward VIII of England abdicate the throne in the thirties. A woman like her, whose story was colored by the distance of fame and history, could provoke a constitutional crisis in the name of love, and still be celebrated as a heroine. In constrast, ordinary women who wrote to *Vosotras*, had to behave, and avoid burdening their husbands too much. Passionate love, therefore, became a fantasy, a desire, but was not yet a legitimate option for a "respectable" young woman.

I get a feeling[8] that as the sixties went by and even more so at the start of the seventies, these cracks became deeper, especially in outlets targeted to "young modern women" like the magazine *Claudia*,[9] founded in 1957. The journalists who answer readers' questions for the agony aunt column begin to use phrases like "listen to your heart," when it comes to romantic decisions, instead of the preceding favorite "listen to your mother." And even more so, the "offering of love" (or the idea of the "proof of love") begins to appear as permission to engage in premarital sexual activity, wiping out the previously unbreakable idea of the importance of practicing celibacy until marriage. There is still a long way to go for mass media to be able to speak openly about female desire and pleasure, but the fact that romantic love worked for the women of those times as a legitimate discourse to exert sexual freedom is not a detail of minor importance—even if sexuality was thought of only in terms of offering something to a man (which today is neither modern nor feminist). It's hardly surprising that women brought up with outdated values consider these ideas of love and passion as freeing and subversive.

What happens to the men? Within the context of melodrama, they also clash with their families to be with the girl of their dreams, however, the image of masculine freedom runs on different tracks. I intuit that this has to do with a key difference: romantic love offered many women words to be able to speak, though in a foggy and heteronormative way, of their own desire and act upon it. Men did not need it to be able to do so. They were permitted to exert their sexuality freely even before marriage, outside of it, and at any time, hence they did not need to relate (like women did) the search of love to freedom or courage.

While male courage is culturally linked with war, sports, and politics, female courage is collectively thought of as linked with loving a man. There is a myriad of examples, but a recent one can be seen in the songs of Gilda,[10] most explicitly in "I do not regret this love" and "Brave heart." The latter one goes:

I knew I loved you on day one,
And my loving soul cries in secret,
Your wandering love leaves me breathless,
Because I know you will never, ever be mine.
I drank your poison and fell into your trap,
They say that you just play games,
And I think all you do is make me suffer,
And I will fall into the depths of hell.
But I don't care at all as I want nothing at all,

I only want to feel what my heart yearns for.
And I don't care at all, as I want nothing at all,
And I will learn how much it hurts the soul to say goodbye.
Because I have a brave heart
I will love you, I will love you,
Because I have a brave heart
I'd rather love you and lose you.

In the movie *Gilda, no me arrepiento de este amor* (2016) directed by Lorena Muñoz and starring famous Argentinian actor Natalia Oreiro, Gilda gives up her job as a kindergarten teacher to attend dance parties despite half-hearted resistance from her husband, whom she ends up leaving to be able to continue doing what she loves: singing. It's not that falling in love isn't brave. But none of the other much braver things that Gilda did, other than falling in love, appear in these beautiful songs we still dance to today. Aside from the stylistic conventions of the music genre cumbia, I believe that it is clear that thousands of women across all decades did things that were just as brave, or even more so, than fighting for love. They raised children alone, they fought with their families to pursue their dreams or earn their own money, they ran away from their homes to live on their own terms. But the revolution the world allowed them to tell, to sing, was that of having a heart that is brave enough to love and to lose. Or, in other words, having the freedom to choose to give themselves to a man.

When I said that the religion of my friends, at the time I met them having just abandoned Judaism, was love, I was referring to all of this because the conceptual engine of romantic love is in excellent working condition. The issues and adversities love encounters today are different to those of the sixties—sexual revolution and a revolt against mass media consumption, not to mention the internet—but, despite all this, romantic love (its ghost) continued and continues to live and circulate among us and in our fantasies. While boys defied adults by getting into fights or consuming drugs, our preferred form of transgression related to sex and men, more specifically to the "wrong" men—which at a time when we had less prohibitions than previous generations, meant falling for unsuitable men or for someone much older. I don't mean to say that all our relationships were like this, at least not all the ones I had were. Nor do I regret many which were, though I could have done without certain forms of violence that I experienced or at least I could have recognized them as such instead of accepting them in the name of living an "intense love affair" with an "intense lover." But the image that comes to mind now is not that of a violent scene, but one that lies in a rather grey area. My mother suggested that I go out with my friends on a day when I wanted to stay at home because—I'm not sure if she knew or suspected it—I was waiting for a call from a boy (it was 2004 and I still didn't own a cell phone). To help me integrate with the girls from my new secular high school, my mother had quickly abandoned all the morals imparted on her during her upbringing. Yet, she retained an intuition (something that would take me a long time to understand): in life, men should never be too important. It had been a few hours since the girls had written to me suggesting we go to the cinema to watch a movie we long wanted to see. I was sure that my mother didn't understand anything about love; that it wasn't true that a man didn't care about you if he left you waiting at home; "he's an artist," "he gets easily distracted," "he doesn't follow time," "all the men who are worth a dime are like that." That night I didn't argue with my mother so that she would let me go out dancing, we argued so that she would let me stay in my room, staring at the ceiling, biting my nails, and waiting for the manifestation of someone else's desire.

Towards the end of the nineties, New York-based photographer Justine Kurland presented a series of photographs of teenagers that were seen all around the world. I saw them in 2018, in an article in *The New Yorker*, and I was surprised the photos were as old as they were. Everything about the energy of these intrepid girls fitted the feminism of the girls who show their bosom on Instagram and cover their nipples to stop the app from taking them down. In one of the photographs, you can see two girls in an alleyway behind a huge toy store. They have impatient looks on their faces and are holding a bottle inside a brown paper bag. In another, three girls are talking in what looks like a school restroom: one is sitting on the toilet smoking, the other two look at her, one has no shirt on and the other isn't wearing trousers. There are more photographs: on the road, in the mountains, girls trying to pee in the middle of the forest. When I think of the common denominator, the thing that's so special about them, I realize that these images are unusual. We're used to seeing boys in these situations, behaving like "rebels without a cause," defiant, expressing a kind of violence. The prototype of a wanderer and a bohemian is historically masculine. There is no female equivalent in pop culture, or at least in mass media culture. There is no female version of James Dean. It's not that these figures have not existed: Janis Joplin, for example, could have played this part. But a woman who lets loose is, by common sense, a wreck. And such a woman, unlike her male counterpart, is not an object of desire, but an object of pity. In the collective imagination, the true, glamorous and sensual rebel girl is someone else: the one with her arm around the waist of the boy on the bike.

D uring my first decade in the secular world, from the age of twelve until the age of twenty-two, I didn't have any expectations for my future. I still lived at my mother's house in Once and didn't quite know to what extent I would be able to deviate from the path that had already been laid out for me, the path that was supposedly right for me. My elementary school classmates had all followed that path and were a constant warning for me: that world was still out there, all around me, and if I pulled away too hard, I could get dragged back in like in a nightmare. I watched them marry boys they had known for three months and had never kissed. I watched them fall pregnant one year, and again a year after that, and the next one, their backs aching from carrying big bellies, babies, and pushing strollers. I heard them talk about recipes and ways to get rid of stains, their lives completely decided upon by the time they were nineteen years old. For better or for worse, they didn't expect anything other than to raise their children and then watch history repeat itself, that was all.

When I bumped into them and told them about my new school or about university, they looked at me with pity in their eyes, as if I was telling them about a dangerous addiction, then they asked if I at least still went to the synagogue. I told them I did and then carried on walking. Some of them seemed genuinely happy with the lives they led, others didn't. Ultimately, this happens with any way of life chosen, and I no longer judge them like I used to back then, nor do I claim to know everything about their psyche. But I can speak for myself: it was clear to me that what I wanted was to run as far as I could from there, and I was ready to pay any necessary dues to be able to do it.

I think that's why it took me so long to notice the *machismo* present in my new life, despite having read all the feminist theory I could get my hands on and self-proclaiming myself a feminist when I was a teenager. I simply couldn't see it. I know that this blindness has little to do with me and my personal experience. One of the most sophisticated and perverse characteristics of the oppression against women is that violence and pleasure are deeply interwoven in education, in the process of socializing, and in our sexual experiences, so separating them is a lifelong process. Peruvian writer Gabriela Wiener, in her article "The sex of the survivors,"[1] explains this very well. A friend of hers felt deeply upset because the rape stories she read on social media left her horrified, but also aroused her. When she asked Wiener if she believed her to be a monster, Wiener replied that she did not. That is how we were brought up; so that the same thing that makes us feel violated, makes us feel desired, because that is the image of sex that we've been sold and that we know of, even if we have never been victims of rape. I recognize my teenage self in this story. I remember not knowing how to feel when a man followed me for fifteen blocks, if I should be afraid that he would follow me all the way to the door of my house or flattered because he found me sufficiently attractive to *take the time* to follow me. I also remember thinking, when a man in a suit around thirty years of age cornered me outside school in the Tribunales area, that I had to swallow my fear because I was the one who had asked for my school uniform skirt to be shortened because I loved showing my legs. It's not that I was blaming myself. I didn't think it was my fault or anyone else's. "These are the consequences of living in a free and sexualized world; if you don't like it, you can go back to Once," I would tell myself. Of course, I didn't want to do that, so I was left with the other only option: toughen up, relax my jaw, and smile at the man while he forced himself against me. *Thank you for your interest, come back soon.*

I do not know if it was my age or the security of knowing no one could make me go back to my old life, but when I turned twenty-two, something in me clicked. Beyond my own world, times were changing. In 2011, the Buenos Aires version of the internationally recognized blog *Hollaback!* was born. There, groups of women from different cities came together to share their stories of sexual harassment on the streets and invited other women to send theirs. I read about them in "Las 12," a supplement of Argentinian left-wing magazine *Página/12*, and immediately joined the feminist blogging sphere, which had been around for a few years. These women were not Virginia Woolf or Simone de Beauvoir, nor were they the great philosophers I had been reading in print, but ordinary girls like me, and they were recognizing violence in situations I considered normal and acceptable. I stopped thinking about each specific anecdote and once I began reading, I felt that I was witnessing something that went far beyond them towards a point of no return. The violence we suffered from an early age on the streets and everywhere else led women to develop a very specific relationship with public spaces, with the night, and with the world in general. Spaces that, for a man, were like amusement parks, were minefields for us. And until that conversation started on the internet, many of us accepted it as if it were nothing more than an unavoidable geographical accident.

The following year, I began working at the Fundación para el Estudio e Investigación de la Mujer (FEIM, Organization of the Study and Research of Women), a non-profit feminist organization led by old-guard activist Mabel Bianco. I assisted her and other activists who were a few years older than me, I went to meetings and took notes, I edited and wrote bills or requests for information that would be presented alongside other organizations' requests. I also helped organize events for young activists from all over the country. Mabel must have been around seventy years old and had a few decades of activist experience on her shoulders, but she would still sit down to discuss matters with girls my age or even younger, treating us as equals. I couldn't understand her at first, she was very strict but she didn't want me to do my job quietly—quite the opposite. She would often call me to her office, and I would go, fearful of having done something wrong with a report, but Mabel only wanted to show me something she had been writing or reading and ask me what I thought of it. If we went to a meeting with legislators (I remember a particular one with Argentine politician María Jose Lubertino), where I was the youngest and least experienced attendee, she would always ask for my opinion, as if it mattered as much as everyone else's. She was never too busy. When we had visits from young activists—boys and girls who were risking their physical integrity by going to the only gay club in their cities to hand out condoms—she would always drop everything to listen to them quietly. For Mabel, young girls weren't just our "target population" as we referred to them in the forms we filled out for UNESCO; they were colleagues, they were soldiers who fought on a battlefield she wanted to understand better.

One of the main goals we worked towards during the year I spent at FEIM was raising awareness about "violent relationships"—the way in which adolescent and young women generally experience gender violence in contrast to the notion of "domestic violence" or "violence within the family" evoked by older women. The campaigns, activities, and the outreach materials we created aimed to evidence how certain attitudes that are perceived as acceptable—for example, your boyfriend wanting to check your phone, speaking badly of your girlfriends, asking you to "prove your love," or not wanting to wear a condom—are, in reality, signs of violent relationships.

In general, our articles intended to disarm romantic love of its most traditional weapons to move away from the paradigm of offering everything so that a man can occupy one-hundred percent of the space in your life. After reading these pieces and discussing them with other activists, I recognized very similar situations to my own and my friends'. But although many girls my age and of my generation could relate to these stories of sacrifice, I felt that many of us had put up with bad treatment and violent attitudes without necessarily ascribing to the most traditional idea of romantic love and complete surrender, even explicitly rejecting it. All of us had other things going on in our lives, we worked and studied, some had children, we all had friendships to take care of; we all said that our friends were very important, that we wanted to be independent, that we knew we didn't deserve violence. The message "you are worth more" that I read in the leaflets seemed obvious and redundant, something I already knew, yet I still found myself in many of those situations we catalogued as violent. For example, I had done many things I didn't want to do so that my boyfriend would not leave me, even though he had never threatened to do so (if fixing the patriarchy does not start with the individual, it is for this reason: even without a direct threat, a woman who has internalized this "message" feels disciplined. She understands that, if she says "no," there's a possibility of him leaving and so she has to behave accordingly to avoid that). I had let men in clubs mistreat me, and (I am ashamed to admit) I had made fun of girls who resisted, who suffered or would not put up with the same treatment because—becoming one with patriarchal culture—I considered them soft, not very streetwise, little girls (which was the worst thing you could be). I didn't believe that men had to be the center of my life nor that it was worth offering my whole self to one (least of all to just one), but I still found myself always choosing to go out with a guy rather than with my friends (often regretting it afterwards), sleeping with men who I didn't really like just so they would call me again (why did I care so much if we stopped seeing each other if I didn't particularly like them?), and putting up with horrible situations just to get approval from others—though that rarely happened. This was not just about violence, but also about making decisions I didn't feel completely comfortable with but was unable to avoid.

Not long ago, a young woman from a writing course I regularly attend read a story about her experience at twenty-two or twenty-three years old when she slept with a man she didn't like without there being any form of violence involved. All the men in the room thought it very strange, as if there had been a mistake, an incoherence in the plot, but all the girls recognized this as something that happens often, though none of us could put into words why.

Two moments are directly linked in my memory, two simultaneous realizations. Firstly, that my voice mattered. That it was up to me, to us, to sit down and consider the new, specific, and unique ways in which societal constructions about love oppress us today, even if we weren't Simone de Beauvoir or Virginia Woolf. That Mabel was not just listening to me as a favor, but because, effectively, patriarchy always renews itself and we must continuously rethink everything. Secondly, that the traditional tale of romantic love was still solid but that, in the dawn of the twenty-first century, I couldn't explain why, for my friends and for myself, it was so important to be with a man—to feel his gaze and approval, to show the world that we were women who were capable of being desired by a man and keeping his attention on us no matter what. As the second decade of the twenty-first century began, the image of women as eternal housewives and selfless mothers that I had seen in Once seemed like science fiction for my friends from the secular world; similarly, the version of romantic love as a sacrifice, even if we had learned it during our adolescence, already seemed outdated, childish, and foreign.

However, the idea that attracting and keeping a man was somewhat vital for a woman's happiness, still survived among us, always renewing itself and remaining relevant.

Half a century after the sexual revolution of the sixties, the mandate of the long-term monogamous relationship as the path that warrants happiness is still alive, particularly for women.

In big cities, an increasing number of people live alone,[2] but there is still a lot of stigma associated with single women—any woman who does not have a partner and is around thirty years old can confirm this. A young woman wrote to the newspaper where I run the agony aunt column:

> I am twenty-five and feel like gatherings with friends and family are torture. At eighteen I had my first boyfriend then broke up with him six months later. After that, I met many boys who I was attracted to (to varying degrees) or liked enough for it to develop into something more. But it was the same story with all of them, we met up, had a good time together, but no one wanted to take it further. I was simply "cool."
>
> I spent a long time wondering what the problem was, or if it was me. I believe myself to be pretty and am almost one-hundred percent sure that I have a lot to offer, but it seems that no one is interested in seeing that . . .
>
> I ended up often thinking that perhaps it's because I agree to have sex "too fast" and should play hard to get instead . . . because, culturally, that's what's acceptable if you want someone to respect you and want something more with you. But that's not who I am, and I don't think that suppressing my sexual desire should make me a better or worse person.
>
> Going back to the beginning . . . in all gatherings, I get asked why I don't have a boyfriend, and this makes me feel incredibly hopeless because I feel that a "boyfriend" isn't just something you pick up in the supermarket (though I would like to be able to purchase one to avoid these questions), and because I don't have an answer. The worst thing is that I have to put up with comments

like: "you'll never find a boyfriend if you're like that," and I don't feel that I'm very different to people who are in a relationship . . . I have a strong personality, but I'm not an ogre, I'm a lot more charming than a lot of people I know, but it seems like that doesn't count when getting someone to fall in love with me.

I'm scared of being alone forever . . . not only because I feel the pressure of having to have a partner, but also because I would like to fall in love again and experience a reciprocal and honest love . . . there's nothing better than that.

How can I make myself and others around me feel less anxious about this?

Thanks,

Forever Single (25)

The hypocrisy that characterizes the discourse of romantic relationships is not new. What is new is the way in which this narrative is articulated in relationships between people and, as a result, the extent to which we feel or do not feel this mandate governs us. Some of this can be read in the way "Forever Single" struggles to directly name what she is feeling, rejects it as an external pressure (though she does recognize that family gatherings are torturous), and separates herself from others around her as if they were unconnected and different issues.

No one, or almost no one, would say today that it is "mandatory" to have a partner to take Instagram pictures with, laughing at nothing and lying on incredibly white sheets, or eating avocado on toast. No one would say it's immoral not to do this or that your family will stop talking to you if you don't (which could happen in the neighborhood where I come from if you decide to deviate from the norm). Equally, no one would put a gun to your head to force you to be skinny and successful. Our mothers do not teach us how to become a good girlfriend, wife, or woman. Because none of this happens, we tend to think that we are completely free and that, if we do not feel we are, it is due to our own weakness; that if we begin to "think differently" we will stop suffering for being too fat, single, or not earning enough. I have some good and some bad news: Firstly, you are not alone; all that you consider to be your own fault is not within your control (it only appears to be); secondly, the "problem" will not be fixed with a change in your thinking. What needs to be fixed is the world.

Just because no one is pointing a gun to our heads and telling us to find a boyfriend, doesn't mean that there is not a system that conditions us; a system that does not outright forbid us from choosing but instead makes certain choices more costly, in either financial, symbolic, or emotional terms. Although laws that regulate, for example, maternity and paternity leave contribute to an unfair distribution of childcare responsibilities, it would be difficult to affirm that written regulations alone determine the unfair distribution of labor. There are no laws that are conducive to making women dedicate more time and effort to housework such as cleaning or cooking and yet that is the way things are everywhere in the world.[3] The symbolic structures in which we place women do not only live in our imagination. They are concepts with real and material consequences. In *The Feminine Mystique*,[4] the 1963 classic that many believe to have inaugurated the second wave of feminism, Betty Friedan calls the construction of an ideal woman that limits the options of real women *the feminine mystique*. With this book, feminism embarks on a process that is essential for us to remember and update: calling out the way in which patriarchy is not only prohibiting, but also enticing.

First-wave feminists had focused on the explicit restrictions women faced. What Friedan and her contemporaries exposed were the various ways in which the patriarchy proposes models of identification and happiness (for example, being a wife and a mother is the only option for a good life and all other intentions are distracting and of little value for women) that are as important as written prohibitions when it comes to women's freedom, though these are often harder to visualize and to deconstruct. Patriarchy does not only interfere with our behaviors, but also with our desires, our dreams, and our aspirations. Philosopher Silvina Álvarez explains that it undermines our autonomy by shaping our understanding of society and, consequently, conditions our beliefs about the options available to us.[5]

The fact that going to university is legal, for example, is not enough to make someone *go* to university. Other material and symbolic conditions must be met. During my childhood, I witnessed this clearly as Once, after all, is still located in Argentina. Aside from certain obstacles such as having lectures on Saturdays or finding *kosher* food during school breaks, it is permissible and conceivable for girls like my primary school friends—Orthodox Jewish girls growing up in the low/middle class, daughters of tradesmen and housewives—to attend university. But why do only very few do it? It's not forbidden (though parents would not hesitate in doing so if one of their daughters were to suggest it) but no one ever mentions it. There are no role models or referential figures who point female desire in that direction.

The postmodern and liberal West also operates in this way, though less evidently. The mechanism has somewhat been exacerbated in recent years. In a culture like ours—saturated with images and discourse—what is not shown or mentioned does not exist, which is a perverse particularity. The people who sell the image of the perfect couple in the media of your choice are not celebrities or influencers, but your own friends, and it could even be you depending on how happy or insecure you feel in that particular afternoon. We are the ones who choose to show our beauty and how in love, successful, or glamorous we are; we choose to turn portions of our lives into something spectacular (a *spectacle*) that is worth watching; we determine which aspects of our lives or which moments are not worth remembering and allow them to fade into oblivion. We all know Instagram is not reality and that we "edit" our experiences, but that is the small print: effectively, we willingly consume this fiction and end up believing it. The only lives full of problems I know of are my own and my friends'; of the rest, I only see the ideal profile of a life full of romantic meals out and passionate kisses on heavenly beaches. Am I the only one who argues with her boyfriend? Am I the only one who goes weeks without having or wanting to have sex? Am I the only one who suffers from insomnia due to the fear of losing my job? Deep down I know I can't be the only one. I then think of Forever Single, who is four years younger than me. Her Instagram must be plagued with couples trekking the Inca Trail, bare feet in the sand of the beaches of Villa Gesell, and girls dancing in a club who "at least" are enjoying single life more than she is. I need someone to tell her the truth, that the couple on the Inca Trail cannot stand each other, that the couple in Villa Gesell keep wondering what it would be like to go on holidays without each other, and that those girls dancing happily on our feeds also, every now and then, feel lonely and unsatisfied.

So how does the ideal of monogamy work today? What sets it apart from the ideal of monogamous relationships of the fifties, which second-wave feminists wanted to cast aside? And why, with everything that has happened in-between, is it still alive and valid for so many women? In research work carried out by philosophers, sociologists, and historians, in conversations among friends, and in the letters I receive for my column at the newspaper, I keep finding the same questions that resist clear answers. The most intimate, deeply rooted, and invisible points slip through my fingers every time I feel I've grasped a clear and truthful answer. But, standing on the shoulders of giants, I want to lose the fear of being wrong and attempt to be explicit.

At its worst, the ideal couple of our time is a lot more similar to the one of previous decades than we believe. Like most people who live in large cities, I spend a considerable amount of time on the internet, reading about what is expected of me: what I should do, what I should love, what I should eat. In summary, *lifestyle* content that is still mostly targeted at women, the safekeepers of private life. The first thing that's clear is that leading a public life (work and community as well as political, social, and financial participation at a larger scale than within their homes) becomes impossible if women are to take having a *good lifestyle* seriously. Living well is costly (though it seems impossible to be able to earn all that money if we are focusing on "living well"), time-consuming, and laborious. We need to dedicate time to cooking, decorating our house, working out, meditating, tidying up our wardrobe—as Mary Kondo recommends—recycling, connecting with nature, and of course, working on our relationship. The second obvious point is that, in contemporary urban consumer societies, romantic relationships are another chore. On *Goop* (Gwyneth Paltrow's lifestyle platform and the contemporary bible), the section dedicated to "relationships" is under the "work" tab. While the first of these two discoveries highlights the likeness between our universe and that of the girls who used to listen to radio shows while embroidering, the second one discusses a novelty that is specific to our time: that romantic relationships are yet another job among the many that an urban capitalist society imposes on us. The romantic relationship, we are told, requires a huge amount of effort, though one never questions whether it is worth the exertion nor how the labor invested on this effort is distributed between the two genders.

For our grandparents, and to a certain extent, for our parents (depending on their age and whether they are part of the transitional generation), work was work and family was family. Worrying about maintaining romantic relationships is a recent phenomenon. Women's magazines in Argentina during the fifties and sixties might have discussed marriage, but not the notion of "couple" (though sometimes the word is used as a synonym of marriage, it is never used as a headline for example). Yet advice for overcoming "marital problems" does not appear as often as it does in the press of the eighties and the nineties. A lot has happened since then, the sexual revolution, the contraceptive pill, the incorporation of women in the workforce, and the legalization and mass acceptance of divorce. Prior to that, when separating or being single were not socioeconomically valid options, no one thought to question monogamy, infidelity, or how to carry the weight of routine on their shoulders. These were shameful and immoral issues with no real solution. Once divorce begins to appear as a viable alternative (not just legal and possible, because it already existed and happened often, but also acceptable in a symbolic and financial sense), the couple and the family begin to be considered as different entities that, though not completely detached, are characterized by a certain independence. New acceptable ways to be in a couple also emerge. Those who live together but are not married and don't have children are no longer elicit pity or shame. Premarital sexual relationships are no longer taboo but have become the standard norm instead, and as part of a transformative process lasting decades, courtships become longer and more meaningful. This stage is no longer seen as the prelude to marriage but as an entity carrying its own weight; in fact, today, most of the communications targeting young women speak of "your partner," "your boyfriend," or "your man" instead of "your husband" or "future husband."

On the other hand, freedom directly influences our expectations. We all (women, men, and those who do not identify with either of these terms) expect a lot more from a relationship than previous generations did. It was not just divorce that led to this process of "amplification" of our ambitions but also new conversations focusing on sexuality and women's increased ability to seek out pleasure and make sense of other spaces (professional, educational, artistic, and political) outside of the family, as well as the increasingly generalized idea (historically supported by alternative and, later, mass media outlets and consumer society) that the search for pleasure and fun is a reasonable aspiration and not a sinful impulse that must be resisted. Some marital issues we talk about today have always existed in the context of silent shame that turned them into social taboo, but others emerged because of these changes. The question of how to avoid the routine that marks monogamous relationships (a question that women's magazines answer in unison "with blood, sweat, and tears!") illustrates a problem characteristic of a society that has, fortunately, recognized pleasure and fun as legitimate aspirations and that, at the same time, presumes to fix everything without returning to old inequalities (a man can freely exert his sexuality outside of marriage, but a woman has to suppress hers while looking the other way) or putting too much pressure on bourgeois couples and families. Thus, new relationships are formed simultaneously with these issues.

This freedom was not distributed equally or, at least, it did and does not have the same consequences for everyone. Once maternity is involved, a woman's romantic decisions are hugely limited by her income. The availability of tangible and symbolic life projects alternative to being a mother and wife is also linked to socioeconomic conditions. However, this does not mean that the ideal of the perfect couple only operates within the lower and middle classes; aspirations are not limited to those who can effectively achieve them but are instead established as general objectives for everyone.[6] Although, empirically, there is still a lot of research to be done on these intersections and, in particular, on the way in which they manifest in Latin America in general as well as specifically in Argentina. There is no doubt that these ideals take form and are experienced in different ways depending on the specific context and social strata.

Although my personal experience is in the urban middle class, it is not true that struggling to adhere to the prevailing ideals surrounding love, romantic relationships, and the family structure is an issue that is exclusive to a certain social stratum. Many women aspire to form the perfect couple and travel to Mexico or have a beautiful baby to exhibit on Instagram—including those who do not have a partner, a uterus, or money to pay for the flights. Nor is it true that women with fewer resources do not have time for this "nonsense" because they are too preoccupied with bringing food to the table. In general, they end up juggling their time between this nonsense and the more vital matters, without ever coming up for air, which becomes yet another way—a particularly cruel way—of trapping them within their own subjective desire.

The discourse surrounding the "couple" as labor is all around us and reaches different women in various ways in socioeconomical terms. A relationship is no longer something that looks after itself: passion has to be nurtured and one has to communicate, share, make time for it despite being tired or overwhelmed by other activities (often imposed by the need to survive) including childcare, professional and other obligations (friendships and hobbies are not even included in this equation as they are considered less crucial in the making of a "fulfilled" woman). There is a valid point in this discourse that relates to a call for honesty as well as to the experience of the first generation of mass divorcees: maintaining a relationship is not easy. But there is a conjecture behind this way of thinking that is rarely explicit; the idea that our happiness is something that we can control and that depends on our willingness and decisions. If a woman wears a bunny outfit twice a month, spends twelve hours a week in the gym for the rest of her life, invests twenty percent of her salary in treatments or make-up to not "let herself go," works day and night to be able to afford that romantic weekend getaway, reads enough books on emotional intelligence; in summary, if she does her "homework," this undertaking called the relationship cannot go wrong. Capitalism no longer speaks to us about the Christian idea of women sacrificing themselves for their homes or for love (of course there are enclaves where these ideals are still present, but in generational terms they are no longer relevant); capitalism talks to us about effort, labor, and even merit. Maintaining a relationship in the twenty-first century is a thing of merit, something only "the best of us" can achieve. Of course, like everything when it comes to meritocracy, it requires time and money; many even speak of "investments"—keeping the fire burning is an investment, as if a relationship was the stock market. Monthly or every other month, an article is published that explains why millennials have less sex than previous generations, that our relationships are colder, that we are all going to die alone and that we can blame the internet or postmodernism or the moral crisis, depending on who is writing. I cannot recall reading about the difficulty of maintaining a high libido in the context of job insecurity we live in; with the many thousands of side jobs that we must take on, rent we have to pay, and no guarantee of a good night's sleep or the space to desire in peace. Nor can I recall reading about how the decomposition of the old familial and community ties (oppressive, no doubt, but also comforting) adds pressure to the romantic relationship by being one of the few support pillars still standing in a context in which the competitive and cruel ethos teaches us that contemporary capitalism does not support the construction of new support networks.

Suddenly, your partner must satisfy all your needs: they should be your best friend, your confidant, the father of your children, your travel companion. There are no issues you cannot discuss with them, no places you would rather visit with someone else, no life events you would not want to share with them. They become your whole universe. I am surrounded by people who are self-proclaimed "progressives" and still give me recriminatory looks when I choose to go to an event with a friend instead of with my boyfriend; when I "let" my boyfriend go out dancing alone to a party with his friends; when I gladly accept the offer of a work or academic trip, which would mean spending several weeks away from him. Examples like these that transgress the idea of a partner as your whole world generate reactions that, on days of low self-esteem, make me doubt the love I feel towards my partner. I understand that for some people, this absolutist approach to couple life works, but why should it work for all women with no exceptions? And why, if it does not work for me, should I think that I am doing something wrong, that my love only goes halfway because I am not putting enough "effort" into it?

It's easy to buy into the idea that with hard work everything is possible and that no one can stop you. The alternative, accepting that there are too many factors in love (material, financial, and political, as well as personal and random factors) that do not depend on either your diet or your emotional abilities would be more upsetting. Thinking that if we dedicate enough of our resources to building a relationship, it *must* work out, gives us hope. Particularly in a world in which a good relationship is still synonymous with success and a woman who cannot manage to build one, like the girl who wrote in to the agony aunt column, is a failure.

Conjugal harmony, which used to be a moral mandate, has been recycled as a parameter of success. It is clear that the ideal changes. Gender norms today appear to be less clear—though, in practice, the division of work in terms of gender still exists—as raising children within a civilized family is not the only thing that matters; new requirements concerning pleasure appear (a couple must have a good sexual relationship and, as far as it is possible and without crossing any lines, this needs to be apparent) and requirements concerning leisure (the collection of experiences such as travelling, eating out, going to the cinema and the theatre, or going to a football game of the team of your choice). Nonetheless, certain things such as monogamy remain intact. Open relationships with diverse sexual agreements or with more than one permanent partner undoubtedly exist, but they are still an oddity discussed mainly in the pages dedicated to trends and news.

Once the idea of maintaining a marriage as a moral duty loses validity, the importance of the component of "happiness" as a state of pleasure and constant joy becomes hyperbolic. If your partner does not make you happy around the clock, it means your relationship isn't working and you must discard it as if it was a disposable plastic cup; if you experience moments of doubt, dissatisfaction, or boredom, you are underperforming in the area of love. No one truly lives like this but as this is what we showcase on social media and in conversations, we end up feeling that other people do live like this and that, perhaps, "you can also find something better." Eva Illouz[7] explains, without explicitly referencing social media (but referencing popular dating services in the United States), how this idea of "finding something better" characteristic of the contemporary world conspires against happiness in a relationship. We find ourselves constantly comparing our relationship not only with those of people we know or believe to know, but also with the ideal of an unassailable contender who could be "out there" waiting for us. Eva Illouz believes this to be one of the many consequences of the deregulation of what she calls the market of love: once the rules of who can partner up with whom are relaxed (a man can marry his secretary without her "lower social rank" causing tongues to wag; though the opposite scenario would be, of course, much harder), the "fish in the sea" multiply exponentially. Illouz is right, of course, but in the twenty-first century, the mantra of "one can always be better" fits a more ample narrative which goes beyond love and romantic relationships.

In the last ten years, at least, well-being became a kind of competition reminiscent of *The Hunger Games*. Talking to women of my mother's generation or who are older than me, I realize that there is something about this phenomenon which is quite recent. The preoccupation with one's health was not what it is today (countless women of that generation smoke even though they've known since the eighties that it's detrimental to their health). It's true that they would follow strict diets, but without making the suffering evident. They also never concealed the fact that being married was difficult, that getting a divorce was difficult, that working all day and returning home to care for their children was difficult, essentially, that everything was difficult. Although the majority (of course, there were dissidents) did not question these duties, at least they never denied them. I find this same ideal in *Having it All: Love, Success, Sex, Money . . . Even if You're Starting with Nothing*, the book of life advice which *Cosmopolitan* editor Helen Gurley Brown published in 1982. "I think you may have to have a tiny touch of anorexia nervosa to maintain an ideal weight . . . not a heavy case, just a little one!" writes Gurley Brown in prose reminiscent of *Sex and the City*.[8] It may sound cruel, but at least she is more honest than the wellness Instagrammers of today who showcase their abs, hard as a rock, and tell me that if I give up gluten, I will feel much better and turn into a goddess just like them, without much effort or extraordinary suffering.

On the one hand, an increasingly large portion of our existence (including our emotional and sexual lives) is becoming public, as if suddenly we were all celebrities presenting our partners in society and announcing separations in solemn declarations to the press. On the other hand, the wellness industry capitalizes on turning everything into a competition, into something that can always be improved. Today, not even leisure, sex, and friendship are free of an obsession for measurement and productivity—one must leverage time destined for resting; failing to do so is a kind of immorality, an unforgivable *waste* we pay for in guilt and angst. None of these mandates leave room for disruption. Sex equals health, having a nap equals health, being in a happy couple equals health. Is there anything better than health in this life? Do you not want to be happier than you already are? Do you not want to live longer? Do you not want to be better? Philosopher Slavoj Žižek talks about the imperative of joy as the idea that being happy today has more to do with the obligation of desire. Is it possible to break away from this? Can we want something other than to be happier than we already are?

One thing must remain clear, between a society that considers good sex a healthy habit and one that considers it a conjugal obligation, I choose the first option. I prefer to live here; I prefer to live like this: I am a daughter of these times, of urban life, an outsider from Once, but exactly for that reason I believe that we can and must criticize the context in order to be more free.

The permanent scrutiny we live in today is an inexhaustible source of anxiety—we all think we're losing in the race for well-being. I'm tired but I also feel guilty for being tired. The narrative surrounding health and wellbeing as the path that leads us to infinite improvement serves to palliate the anxiety caused by an absence of a shared moral order: uncertainty and the emptiness left by the collapse of other greater narratives. In the secular world, we no longer know what it means to be good, but we know—or believe we know—what it means to always be better. And we will break our backs pursuing that, even if it kills us.

But there is another catch, a worse one. We don't need to change the world to be a little better, as the wellness industry explains, and we reproduce it on social media and in our heads. We don't need to rethink and recreate the way in which women and men relate in an emotional and sexual way, we do not need to build a world in which we do not work ten hours a day to be able to live while dedicating time and space to pleasure. "Don't worry about collective change," the daughters of the Helen Gurley Brown generation say. "Just try this new sexual therapy, this new variety of spinach, this new combination of yoga and Pilates, and I promise everything will be ok."

South Korean philosopher and great thinker of our time Byung-Chul Han said in an interview in 2015[9] that, today, we all avoid suffering for love. "We don't want to be vulnerable, we avoid hurting or being hurt in any way. Love requires a great deal of commitment, but we avoid this commitment, because it leads to injury. We avoid passion, and falling in love hurts too much," Han explains to his interviewers. I imagine Han didn't read Eva Illouz's book *Why Love Hurts*, which I quoted in the previous chapter, and which was first published four years prior to that interview, or perhaps he doesn't have many female friends. Weeks after reading Han's words, I receive this email at the agony aunt column:

Good afternoon, Consuelo. I read your column in the newspaper and decided to write to you as I found it very interesting. My story is as follows, the protagonists are myself and the father of my son. We've been together for a long time, since we were teenagers, and our son is four years old. I forgave many infidelities, including compromising messages and pictures I found. He always said he'd start behaving and, well, I wanted to keep the family together, and I loved him. But the last time it happened, it was different. He stopped showing interest in me, he wouldn't take the initiative to do anything together as a family (we both work all day and only see each other for dinner), and only wanted to go out with his friends when the weekend came. When we reached a point where I had to talk about this, he just told me not to bother him, that he wanted to be left in peace. I spent a few months trying to discuss this because he wasn't interested in how I felt, in what was happening to me. But one day I told him to leave and that I didn't want anything to do with him. I said the only one maintaining this relationship was me and I felt he'd lost all interest in me. Was I right to end the relationship? In truth, I feel I need someone who values me. Thank you!

Determined But Not That Determined (31)

Maintaining a happy relationship in the twenty-first century is effectively hard work but, on top of that, it falls on women's shoulders. This woman's story resurfaces repeatedly in conversations with both people I know and strangers. The male version must also exist, but I haven't heard about it, and I'm not surprised. I don't blame those men who are in a relationship, but only halfheartedly. Why should they work on something they don't want if love isn't mandatory? I believe that Determined But Not That Determined made the right decision; what I wonder is why it's often so difficult, why we go through all the effort of insisting even when we know that the other half of the relationship has thrown in the towel.

There are countless different situations, and it's impossible to account for everything that could happen to a person, but I always come back to the same term in the same spaces: being loved by a man or, at least, appearing to be loved by a man is still what measures the social status of a woman. Not only that, many of us—heterosexual women at least—still find it difficult to relate being single to anything other than a state of anxiety, an emotional lack we must remedy as fast as we can. We can enjoy it for a little while, but it will always be labelled as time off, and particularly as the years go by, the idea of becoming a "pathetic old woman" becomes more tangible. Curiously, this prejudice is not based in reality, not even in our own experiences. It does not matter that our happiest moments happened while we were single, or that the pillars we leaned against were our friends (why not?) or our mothers. A woman without a partner, we automatically think, as instructed by the culture (that is chauvinistic, heteropatriarchal, and conservative) must be lonely, as happiness can only flourish between two people. All too often these conceptual engines lead us to lower our standards, be patient, put up with anything just for that bit longer. The contemporary language of love provides infinite tools to justify this: *betting* on love, *working* on the relationship, putting in that extra bit of *effort*. Or will you give up? Furthermore, when one truly buys into this ideal, it turns into a self-fulfilled prophecy: if I put everything into my romantic relationship and do not nurture bonds based on compromise and affection outside of it, I will be alone when I separate. If I don't build projects (professional, community-focused, creative, or political) that are independent of my partner, my whole life will end up revolving around this man, so I better be infinitely patient with him.

Why bother creating anything if ultimately the only thing that matters to the world is that I get married? One of my university students, from a humble neighborhood in the suburbs of Buenos Aires, knows this question all too well. As she tries to become a nurse, swimming against the current and fighting scarcity, she constantly faces questions from her friends. Why isn't she focusing on forming a family and why is she wasting herself and her fertile years away in this absurd cloister (university, not a convent)? My sister, despite her privileged circumstances, also knows only too well. She can't understand why her marriage was more celebrated than her being accepted to a doctorate in biophysics. Thousands of women who leave their cities, their friends, and their lives to follow their partners around the world and ask themselves if they would do the same for them (spoiler alert: according to statistics, most men would not),[10] also know only too well. Girls who stop doing a sport they like or stop going out with their girlfriends, girls who begin deconstructing their lives to make room for their partner (and join in with *his* plans, because the opposite is harder to negotiate), know only too well. The girls who write to the agony aunt column from all over the country—Jujuy, Santa Fe, Boedo or Belgrano—know only too well. I also know only too well. This is not a psychological or individual matter; friendships, projects, and deconstructing them, don't happen in solitude. It's about making a decision and then making it happen, but it is also about communication, and building and re-building, to then decompose discourses and structures that we ourselves keep repeating and feeding into, and that we use to discipline others as well as ourselves.

# CHAPTER 3
## LOVE SCOUTS

I n Orthodox Jewish communities, everyone dresses in the same way. The more orthodox, the more similar: same socks, same skirt design, and they even style their wigs in the same way. In some ultra-Orthodox communities, they all wear black. In my house, we were modern Orthodox Jews. We wore long denim skirts and sneakers, we covered our elbows and knees to go to school but enjoyed a certain freedom when it came to colors and silhouettes (this was key as, in my community, when girls reached adolescence and began looking for a husband, the best resource for showing oneself without breaking any "skin rules" was wearing a skirt that was the correct length, but very tight, "like a tightly wrapped pork loin" we might have said, if we had known what that was). I remember asking my mother, when I was seven, eight, and eleven years old, why girls who attended more religious temples than ours dressed in dark colors with long skin-colored tights and baggy skirts, like a uniform. I didn't think the rules in the Talmud could be so detailed. "Because they want to," my mother would answer most times. This drove me crazy. Do they all *want* to? Was this a kind of impossible coincidence? I felt insulted that my mother thought I would believe that by pure chance, without coercion, all girls in a community would want the same thing.

I guess that suspicion was based on an intuition about desire that became increasingly crucial: that it's diverse and multifaceted, and that if there's a multitude of people doing the same thing, it's because there's something other than desire in-fluencing them. This was a modern intuition in terms of the Enlightenment: that desire represents the freedom and individ-uality of a person, that *beneath* social constrains there must be something clear and authentic that we can unravel—our real personality and what we "truly" want. Today, I believe this to be more complex. I understand that this vital drive is inter-twined with historical, social, economic, political, and cultural factors; that "desire" is not detached from those conditions, and that freedom, as Sartre explains, can only be understood in a particular situation but never in an abstract way that is im-permeable to the tensions in the world. However, I still hold on to a conviction from those days that I increasingly believe to be true: that although pure desire does not exist, it is worth exploring what we feel we want and daring to think about the historical conditions linked to what we always believed to be a certainty. Feminism is not about questioning other women's desire, it's about encouraging us to question our own desire, however painful, especially when we have a feeling that what we desire is not good for us.

I thought about all of this when I began reading and re-searching various ways of organizing emotional and sexual rela-tionships or, in other words, the alternatives to monogamy that are available. During my research, I remembered those girls from my childhood, all dressed the same. Monogamy might have many advantages and virtues, but what's the probability of it working for all of us, when so many sexual, emotional, and personal dispositions exist? Not very high, I believe, though the immense majority of people I know still plan their lives around a bond that is primal, fundamental, and of a superlative impor-tance that subordinates—and organizes—the rest. To a certain extent, at least.

If we understand monogamy as strictly being "an emotional and sexual life-long relationship," we see that almost no one lives like this anymore; Deborah Anapol,[1] clinical psychologist and one of the founders of the polyamory movement in the eighties, explained that most people who today identify as monogamous practice what she calls serial monogamy: having multiple monogamous and successive relationships that are complemented, or not, with an occasional secret affair (more frequent than most imagine). This "seriality" is probably the biggest and clearest change with regard to the behaviors and traditions of previous generations, which gave divorce a much more negative social value than it has today. In fact, it's not surprising that even young people, who are apparently progressive, lament this change. "Relationships don't last these days," "my grandparents were married for all their lives," and even "love used to be real" are phrases we receive from a generation fascinated with yearning for a past that's often fabricated. Most of us know little of the intimacy in our own parents' relationships, and less so of our grandparents', who also belong to a time when personal concerns were only discussed behind closed doors. However, the hegemony of the couple has been showing cracks for some time, if not from the beginning. Isabella Cosse[2] explains that in the forties, almost one in three children born in Argentina was registered as natural or illegitimate. That figure says a lot about single mothers whose lives were considered of a secondary category; about asymmetric marriages in which the husband would quench his sexual thirst on the down-low and the wife had to turn a blind eye in order to keep her house, have food, and maintain her status as a respectable woman; about marriages that perhaps "in olden days" used to last not thanks to a love that was more solid but to hypocrisy and inequality. Women during the forties asked a lot less from their partners than we believe we deserve today; men took what they wanted, wherever they found it, and assumed their wives would tolerate it.

My generation was raised by women who, despite the

difficulties, began practicing the values of honesty, freedom, and equality. Our parents chose divorce rather than persisting with loveless marriages "for appearances" or "to maintain family unity." Of all the battles the Catholic Church fought and lost in Argentina, none was forgotten as quickly as this one: the consensus that families and children can move past divorce and that, sometimes, divorce is preferable to a loveless marriage. Families that are assembled, disassembled, and reassembled, today are ordinary. Values have changed greatly; families have changed, though to a lesser extent, and couples have changed very little in comparison. Most people still maintain exclusive emotional and sexual relationships in which the couple is the nucleus and the most important bond for both parties (except for their children, if they have any). Perhaps the most pronounced change, as well as the seriality of monogamous relationships, happened in women's expectations.

In the twenty-first century, our romantic ambitions are intrepid. Marrying a good person, a man who brings food to the table, is not enough; a relationship that publicly looks right but makes us miserable is not enough either. We want egalitarian and honest bonds, and we are eager to understand what that means. We also want to fall in love, to have sex, and to be loved; we want stability and adrenaline—the lifeboat and the open sea—, we want everything at the same time. But is it possible to *have* all of that? Or is this a recipe for frustration? Is this an *honest* yearning or a mere aspiration, a desire for completeness? Am I an idiot if I pursue it? Am I a cynic if I give up on it?

Gino is not a friend, but I would say that we are good acquaintances on Facebook. We like each other's posts and share certain concerns about romantic relationships and sexuality. As well as researching, writing and working on a radio, Gino is a developer at *Taringa!*, one of the world's first Web 2.0 sites in Spanish, which continues to gain popularity due to its content and despite the rise of social media. *Taringa!* is linked to *Poringa!*, a community exclusively dedicated to X-rated content. Gino also works there, and I know that pornography is a subject that interests him greatly. Because of this and other conversations I had seen on his Facebook, I dared to assume he would be an advocate for non-monogamous relationships and that, furthermore, he would be willing to talk about his experiences frankly. Not only was he, effectively, in an open relationship—with consensual freedom to have sexual encounters with third parties—but he also suggested I meet up with him and his partner. We arranged to go to a bar in Palermo around midday.

Gino's partner is called Bárbara and works at a bank, so we met up during her lunch break near her workplace. She's my age, a couple of years younger than him, and is undoubtedly pretty. Her style is the one I imagine my teenage emo friends would have if they had been ten years older and worked at a bank; there are a number of black details, an intensely dark lipstick and thick eyeliner, but all very delicately applied. Bárbara isn't shy, but she isn't an extrovert either. She has a deep tone of voice, soothing and nice to listen to. Gino is a little more high-energy and feminine, in the sense that there is a certain freshness about him: he's *girly*, that's the word.

Bárbara and Gino have been going out for a year, though they've known each other for five years. They both studied Science of Communication at the University of Buenos Aires, but met on the internet. They first spoke via Twitter and, from that first interaction onwards, began to see each other at university, then to share classes, and study together. They were friends for a long time. When they met, Gino had a different partner. I asked him if that was also an open relationship. "Today, I would say it wasn't . . . but back then, no idea, I don't know," he answers. Gino and Bárbara spoke to their previous partners about the interest in having an open relationship, but this was the first time they've found someone who understands it in the same way they do. Until they met, their approach had more to do with negotiating and convincing someone who was not fully engaged with that kind of relationship which, they learned from their experiences, normally goes wrong. Gino ended his previous relationship on bad terms, and although his ex knows he is going out with someone, he prefers not to upload pictures with Bárbara on social media ("which is the true way of officializing a relationship these days, right?" says Gino with a smile of resignation). "You have to really want this, you both have to be singing in tune," Bárbara explains, "because if one of the two is more motivated to have an open relationship than the other, that always creates conflict."

When talking about the motivations behind this choice, Gino appeals to honesty: "if you've been in a monogamous relationship for years, you're likely to be unfaithful at some point; I'm sure there are exceptions, but that's been my experience, and infidelity is shit, it sucks, lying and cheating on someone is awful," says Gino. "In a monogamous relationship," adds Bárbara, "you always end up lying or at least hiding truths, things you do, almost certainly, and at the very least, your desires." Honesty comes up constantly throughout the conversation. For Bárbara and Gino, monogamy is tied to lies and concealment. I find it interesting that they talk more about this than about freedom; ultimately, we are all free to cheat in this century. Whoever wants to, can simply do it; an exclusive couple is not necessarily less free than an open one but, for Bárbara and Gino, it is undeniably less honest.

They tell each other everything. I ask repeatedly to see if their expressions change slightly, but they don't: they tell each other everything. They discuss the people they are with, or the ones they would like to be with; but I get a feeling that there is something else, a search for an almost absolute intimacy. Bárbara says this began as an erotic exercise. They would write to each other about what they had done with other people or what they fantasized about. They would also repeat this while they were having sex as a kind of virtual orgy (though they have participated in real ones) full of imaginary yet real characters. This habit stuck and has now become a rule within the relationship: if they hook up with someone else, they must tell each other. "If I find out he's been with someone without telling me, I begin to think something strange is going on, because that's the agreement," Bárbara explains. Neither of them defines the other one as jealous, but there is a mutual agreement that, as I later corroborated with research, is of huge importance for those who practice diverse forms of sexual and romantic openness. Consensual pacts must be respected. Bárbara and Gino—like many other people who are in similar relationships—read, research, and debate the self-imposed rules constantly. The idea is to create agreements that both parties can and want to stick to, to avoid betrayal at all costs. There are as many agreements as there are bonds; many couples they know have the opposite rule: they don't share outside encounters with each other. I ask them what they think about that. "Each of us has to do what works," says Gino, "but it's strange . . . because if it really doesn't bother you that your partner is with other people, why dedicate so much of your energy to not finding out about it?"

From a Marxist feminist standpoint, there's a close relationship between monogamy and oppression. Historian Gerda Lerner[3] explains how in *The Origin of the Family, Private Property and the State*, Engels analyzes "the world historical defeat of the female sex" and how this work became the foundation for Marxist feminists to delve into the idea that men's subjugation of women beginning in the home was as unnatural as the subjugation of capitalism of the working class. Engels' perspective posed many issues. It was founded on questionable ethnographic evidence and substituted empirical sustenance with epochal prejudice. However, it did raise the right issues:

the relationship between emotional bonds and economy, the historicity of power dynamics within what was considered the "private sphere," and an incipient recognition of sexuality and domestic work as "services" offered to men rather than natural functions of women.

Men's subjugation of women, as feminist researchers began reconstructing it, was not a universal truth nor did it have a linear history. In fact, it is believed that in certain Neolithic nomadic societies of hunter-gatherers, the roles of women were crucial. They hunted small animals and gathered food, tasks which were arguably as important, if not more so, for the tribe's survival. In contrast, men exclusively hunted larger animals, a task viewed as more exceptional. In many of these communities, there was a gender division of labor, but not a pronounced hierarchy that indicated which of the two performed more valued tasks. Differences between the sexes in this context are characterized as complementary or, in other words, "different but equal." It's no coincidence that emotional and sexual relationships in these societies were far from current monogamous conventions. Our nomadic ancestors and the relationships they constructed and deconstructed, without any agreements relating to the couple as the nucleus of the family, were perhaps the closest ones to the ideal of "free love" humanity ever witnessed.

The arrival of monogamy is linked to agriculture, sedentary lifestyle, and a more pronounced gender division of labor (where housework, emotional, and sexual forms of labor that fall on women in the home are not even recognized as such), as well as the economic, political, and sexual subordination of women by men—the only ones capable of owning land. Monogamy imposed restrictions: the requirement of celibacy until marriage, exclusivity after marriage, and a permanent disposition to satisfy the other's desire. But this was only imposed on women. Men were always free to manage their emotional and sexual affections outside of the rigid marital contract: Engels already spoke of the key role of prostitution in the construction of a family. If men learned discipline through waged labor, women learned it in the kitchen and in the bedroom.

This control over sexuality is not an accessory, a coincidence, nor a random consequence. It does not respond to a biological or natural need,[4] as some religions preached and preach. It is a historical and political condition men imposed on women. A woman who knows other bodies knows the world. She circulates, experiments, knows what she has and what she could have. She learns about desire, about searching; she learns to ask about the conditions of her own life and to question them, to not take them as a given and unbreakable circumstance. Women's sexual freedom endangers men's capacity to subjugate them. The recognition of women as desiring subjects poses a threat to the system that is founded on their subordination, on unpaid labor, on predictable and disciplined behavior. What for a long time was called *virtue* is not only a moral and religious concept, but also a political and economic one.

This shift in values was manifested in full force during certain historical events that have been documented and analyzed. In *Caliban and the Witch*, historian Silvia Federici[5] explains that the prosecution of witches in Europe and in the New World was a key component in the construction of modern capitalism. Witches represented free, desiring, dangerous women who were often not fit for domestic and sexual life with a man, who shared knowledge outside of the patriarchal institutions that imparted and legitimized knowledge (university cloisters, but also convents), who built communities instead of remaining alone in their homes. They were therefore a walking threat against the patriarchal family, accepted traditions, and the incipient bourgeois ideal of marriage.

Of course, the social regulation of female sexuality was not the only thing that was interposed in the path of our liberation. There were also obstacles to the participation in waged labor and politics, among many others. As Modernism advanced, women began overturning explicit restrictions. They obtained the possibility to perform waged labor outside of the home (yet, as Federici also shows, from a Marxist point of view it is questionable to think of labor exploitation as "liberating"), have their own money, go to university, vote, and organize themselves. The structural transformation, however, was much slower and the heterosexual couple had a key role in this. A significant portion, for example, of the gender pay gap that still exists between men and women can be explained by the difference in the time dedicated to housework.[6] An unemployed man still spends less hours doing housework and reproductive labor than a woman in full-time employment.[7]

I am the first woman in my family to have lived alone and not to have moved from the paternal home to a husband's. Despite the particularities of my upbringing, this is a common occurrence even among my friends who grew up in secular societies: the ones who are not first-generation women living alone, are part of second-generation. Our grandmothers, women born between the decades of the twenties and the thirties, were not allowed to enjoy that level of independence.

When my grandmother found out that I was moving out to go live on my own, she was happy. Going against the religious beliefs of my family, she was always the financial pillar of her home and I believe she liked the idea that I would *have fun* before I got married and formed a family (I suppose she never thought that instead of "before" she could have used "if"). However, this wasn't the story for all my friends: many of them, especially those who came from other parts of the country, had to invest a lot of energy in convincing their parents that living on their own or in a house full of single women was safe.

The idea that the world is not a safe place for women (partially true due to how culture shapes men) has an overwhelming disciplinary effect. It implies that women must not live, travel, or start a business without a man. One point this idea takes for granted is that a woman who does not belong to a particular man, belongs to all men in general: one who does not have an owner is at hand for all, is served on a silver platter for the collective to enjoy. She belongs to whoever takes her first, like a banknote you find on the floor.

In *King Kong Theory*, Virginie Despentes speaks of the way in which the fear of rape shapes female destiny. She even calls for "losing the fear" and accepting rape as the patriarchal rite of passage, but not allowing its ghost to restrict our freedom or corner us into the situation of a frozen victim.[8] This is not just a rhetorical strategy but also a key idea: patriarchy recommends that we devote ourselves to a man to avoid other men's violence. Heterosexual monogamy offers protection, while life on the outside (exploring, either alone or with friends, any sexuality that would mean not compromising with one man) puts you in danger "at your own risk." The link between female sexual freedom and danger is profound and omnipresent. In fact, if we think about it, the only women historically allowed to live among women and without men were nuns, who had renounced carnal pleasure. The respectable alternative to monogamy is abdicating sex.

Curiously, current statistics do not coincide with the fear of social circulation that has been impressed on us from a young age. According to a report from NGO Casa del Encuentro, 2679 women were murdered by men between 2008 and 2017. From that figure, at least sixty-one percent of the murderers were the woman's partner or former partner. In seventeen percent of the cases there was no evidence that corroborated a relationship between the murderer and the victim, and only eight percent of the femicides happened in public. Thus, a considerably smaller number of girls were murdered because they were walking under a bridge in the dark, backpacking, living alone, or even working in sexual labor, than those who were engaged in emotional and sexual relationships with men. Even so, heterosexual monogamy still has a much less dangerous reputation than all these other allegedly risky situations.[9]

But it's not only these fears that conspire against women's possibilities of living without a man. I speak in present tense as this is still something that happens everywhere and, particularly, in my country and city. According to the National Census of 2010, only 29.8 percent of single-occupant homes house women, though there has been an increase (in 2001, the percentage was 22.5). The chances that a woman can enter the stage in which she can experience sexuality (and life in general) without the supervision of her family or of a man, are related to her financial situation. Taking this official data from the Ciudad de Buenos Aires, which has a much larger percentage of single-occupant homes than the national average (always above thirty percent in recent years), we can see that people who live alone in the city have the highest income. Choosing to live alone today seems to be a class privilege, both for women and for men but, if we continue to look closer, we find another significant detail. There are more men who live alone than women in all the age segments of society except for one: people over sixty-five years old. Out of the entirety of women who live alone, 58.6 percent fall within that bracket; of the entirety of men living alone, only 33.4 percent are of that age.[10] This phenomenon is surely multicausal and complex but it clearly highlights that, at the age of caring for another, women tend to live with others but men do not.[11] On the contrary, at the age of needing care, women live alone. In general, when we make vital decisions, we do not suspect how our desire is conditioned by the choices that are available and the choices that we believe to be available to us. We tend to think we are choosing freely whether to live in a couple or alone, to separate, or to form a second relationship and construct it in line with the canon of heterosexual monogamy. Perhaps it seems like I give too much importance to the experience of living alone, but more than the experience, I am interested in the idea of its existing in the horizon of what is possible, in knowing that you have the financial, social, and symbolic possibility of living alone seems to me a key and real detail when it comes to thinking about the ways in which we can experience our sexuality freely. If the only available options for a woman are marriage, a convent, or living with her parents forever—as was the case of my grandmother, who did not even have the option of joining a convent—marriage becomes the most attractive option by process of elimination rather than being a personal decision. Any deflection from these options becomes not only a transgression, but also a luxury. Monogamy is not, then, just an abstraction or a desire, an intellectual or immaterial way of thinking of love. It's an experience that will be different depending on the financial possibilities of a woman, and the social and cultural characteristics of the environment where she grew up. It will be different for the woman who has to work both inside and outside of the home, and for the woman who does not need to work or at least can delegate childcare to someone else (most likely another woman); it will also be different for the woman who faces a situation of violence, discomfort, or simply lack of desire, and has the tools to leave as well as inhabiting a social context that respects and approves her decision.

My friends and I truly believed that our decisions were not being regulated by any of this, and that if we chose monogamy instead of "something else" (those alternatives we had seen on the internet, in a documentary, or even heard about through a friend who practiced or supported this lifestyle) it was because we wanted to rather than because we had been brought up this way or because the world was organized to make some of our options essentially more attainable and socially accepted than others. I believe that many of us already know that we are not

above the statistic, social, and financial realities of the patriarchal history that we've inherited and that is still snapping at our
heels.

In the prologue of the anthology *El amor libre. Eros y
anarquía*,[12] writer and journalist Osvaldo Baigorria speaks of
freedom, but especially, like Bárbara and Gino, of hypocrisy.
"The love that is here being labelled as free," he writes referring to various authors of essays featured in the book, "is one
that questions a double standard of morality, hypocrisy, and
cynicism. As René Chaughi says in *Immoralité du Mariage*: if
two people wish to be united with God as their witness, there
is nothing there to be criticized. On the contrary, the problem
is the hypocritical manner of those who choose to undergo a
religious ritual without having set foot in a church since their
first communion. The lie belongs, in this case, to the enemy's battlefield. The anarchic-erotic activist would be, above
all, a moralist."[13] I understand that the hypocrisy discussed
here manifests itself at different levels. On the one hand, in
a contradiction between what is said and what is done, what
is practiced and what (confusingly) is thought. But also, and
I believe more importantly, in a more profound dissonance.
The honesty Baigorria summons is not only "ideological co-
herence," it implies taking ownership of our own desires, of
our condition as desiring subjects. That would be the anarchic lover's ethics, suppressing oneself would be an inauthentic
way of living. Desire always implies a paradox, we perceive it
as something that happens to us or an accident we face, but
we must take responsibility for it. In the Judeo-Christian monogamous tradition, taking ownership of one's desire means
fitting it into a specific mold and suppressing whatever does
not fit. Conversely, free love sees taking ownership of one's desire as the acceptance of its volatility and of an impossibility of
encasing it in pre-established patterns, and even allowing the

essentially disruptive quality of desire to become the mold and engine of our relationships.

However, committing to one's desire is not enough. Like Deborah Anapol and other activists that I have read, Baigorria seems to be very careful not to let his version of free love be confused with a kind of liberal and individualistic fantasy, an apology for having sex without recognizing the other as a person who is capable of wanting and suffering. "Although the counterculture and liberalism that characterizes the decades of the nineteen-sixties and seventies presented anarchic influences," he says, consciously distancing himself from the hippies of summer of love, "the idea of sexual freedom also aided its fight with certain power devices; it incited the dream of multiple sexual encounters without paying for them (free in the sense of free of charge) and it legitimized the possibility of reducing bodies to objects of desire. Replacing 'love' for 'sex' implied, to a certain extent, a loss of innocence."[14] Free love, as those who defend it say, does not legitimize the playboy fantasy: having sex with inflatable dolls who come when they are called and leave when they are required to. In fact, it is likely that the most complicated part (and at the same time the most interesting one in terms of the emancipation of the subject) lies in taking the other's desire seriously, namely letting go of the conviction that the other belongs to you and trying ways of loving outside of that ideal, without neglecting what Baigorria charmingly calls *loving well*.

Baigorria does not apply a gender to his critique of the liberalism of the decades of the sixties and seventies, but feminists such as Andrea Dworkin do.[15] For them, sexual liberation was understood in androcentric terms. Lesbianism, writes Dworkin in *Right-Wing Women*,[16] was not thought of as "real sex" but as a prelude or entertainment for a man, while male homosexuality was barely tolerated. If a woman did not want to have sex with a man, or many, that negative response was always understood as a manifestation of repression or frigidity. Dworkin speaks of a time I did not experience, but I can imagine what she is referring to. In the twenty-first century, a somewhat feebler version of that ideal (and one partly influenced by the epochal changes concerning gender) of a "freedom imperative" appears together with a much more omnipresent cultural tendency: the will to "have it all" and expect others make do with what they have, a renewed version of what Baigorria called "love that is free-of-charge," instead of "free love." And confusing free love with the consumption of people is not exclusively done by hetero, cisgender men.[17]

When I was twenty-two years old, I left my boyfriend whom I had been seeing for nearly four years. During one of the conversations that led to that outcome, I said to him that what I wanted was "to have the best of both worlds." He did not understand, and I did not want to explain but I can now see very clearly what I meant. When he told me he wanted to throw a party on the day he took his final exam, I said that I would probably have to leave early as I had the birthday party of one of my friends from university. He was not a close friend, he was just another friend, but this was an opportunity to go to a party and "play at being a single woman" with various boys who did not know me. Those are the two worlds that I was referring to: the safety of a stable relationship and trusting that he would always be available for me, and the constant novelty of single life. I thought about it as a dichotomy with no alternatives.

I do not know if at the time I knew anything about open relationships but proposing one or thinking about it did not even cross my mind. I had no intentions of deconstructing and enjoying another person's adventures, like Gino and Bárbara did. Nor was I willing to attend workshops on jealousy like the ones the organization Amor Libre Argentina [Free Love Argentina] offers, or willing to do any kind of subjective work on it myself. I thought that having it all (strongly emphasizing the verb "to have") meant being like a traditional man from the twentieth century, a playboy who has a loving and naïve girl waiting for him at home, and a fun one waiting at the bar. All of them at his disposal, all close at hand. This was the only model of sexual freedom that I knew, an asymmetric and consumerist one, introduced to me by hegemonic masculinity; and I believed that copying it was a feminist reaction: control everything, lie to others, use them like chess pieces. But that desire for dominance over others is far from being feminist, loving, or disruptive behavior. There are few things that are more functional for the dominant system than the desire to use other people and then dispose of them as if they were objects, to then acquire new ones. This is replicating the programmed obsolescence created for cell phones on people and emotions.

Any true relationship—be it an open one, a polyamorous one, or a monogamous one that includes the church and confetti—requires keeping one's egotism in check. Philosopher Harry Frankfurt defines the concept of compromise using the terms of rational choice theory.[18] According to this theory, a rational choice is one oriented to favoring one's own personal situation by maximizing wellbeing, utility, and pleasure. But when one commits to a choice, this means relinquishing the possibility of finding a better option, relinquishing a state of maximum wellbeing that is constant and happens in all places. All agreements, no matter how flexible, require a certain level of self-sacrifice, compromise in the strict sense of the word. Gino and Bárbara have a secret code, which they made use of particularly in the beginning of their relationship, that they call *I have a thing*. If one of them calls or writes to the other, and they are busy with another person, that person must answer "I am in something" so that the caller can relax and not become anxious or worried. These rules do not take away from their freedom since they are the ones who came up with them—they discussed them and can modify them conscientiously. Kant would not like free love, and the anarchists would not like Kant; but I cannot resist remembering the way in which he defined freedom. It is not about having no values, but about living according to the principles that come from within us rather than from the outside: it is writing our own laws for ourselves.

From the point of view of desire, monogamy can be a difficult way of living. The subversive power of desire and its physical and metaphysical relationship with freedom lie in its unpredictability. If it is complicated to say what we want now, establishing what we will want in the future—be it the near or distant future—seems almost impossible. Even if we believe we know what we will want in the future, questions still arise: why do we feel the need to impose a restriction on ourselves, to believe that following our desires implies a transgression and even falling out of love? How does that norm satisfy us? Why did I feel more comfortable, I ask myself, with infidelity (with hypocritical and fictitious monogamy) than with polyamory? When I discuss this with my girlfriends, one answer keeps on coming up: "I could not relax if I thought that he could be with other girls." And "relax" seems to be a key word.

I think of the concept of precarity developed by theoretician Isabell Lorey, who used the ideas of Judith Butler and Jean-Luc Nancy as a foundation. In the first chapter of *State of Insecurity: Government of the Precarious*, Lorey highlights a difference between a precarious condition and precarity. What Butler calls a precarious condition refers to an existential dimension of life: when thinking of ourselves as bodies living in society, all living beings are exposed to death, sickness, and other accidents, but also, more generally, to being in contact with others. The same thing that makes us dependent—and that makes the labor of caring so important, as Lorey says—is what makes us vulnerable. "Precariousness designates something that is existentially shared, an endangerment of bodies that is ineluctable and hence not to be secured, not only because they are mortal, but specifically because they are social."[19] It is an existential, material, and historical position of independence, which can manifest as caring for others or as violence against others.

But there is a second dimension to the precarious which is hierarchical and that, to distinguish it from the precarious condition, Lorey calls *precarity*. It differentiates the lives that must be protected from those that pose a threat, legitimizing the precarious condition of the latter. Lorey explains that "domination turns existential precariousness into an anxiety towards others who cause harm, who have to be preventively fended off, and not infrequently even destroyed, in order to protect those who are threatened."[20] The fear and anxiety that come with this precarious living condition—or rather, thinking of this condition in negative terms and always considering otherness and vulnerability as dangerous—give way to this hierarchy: some lives are deemed precarious, becoming more dangerous and less functional (relating to labor, physicality, and sanitary circumstances) when it comes to protecting others from something no one can protect them from: the contingency of being a body in the world.

Lorey also speaks of the association between the ideal of masculinity and protection ("protective patriarchal masculinities and the correspondingly necessary social and legal guarantee of domination in the private sphere of state protection of the modern (male) individual").[21] I am interested in expanding on this relation and applying it to contemporary sexual and emotional relationships in a way that transcends how they work. The condition of our lives—as women and dissidents but also more generally as young people in big cities—is of course precarious in the first sense but also in the second, and that—as Lorey explains—in the twenty-first century is something not even the middle class can escape from. Cash-in-hand work characterized by uncertain and unsafe work conditions is no

longer only a reality exclusive to those who are in the sector of
society with lower incomes. We all run the risk of losing part
of or the totality of our income daily, of having to move somewhere else or nowhere else, of falling out of the system. Yet we
don't live outside of it, we live within its limits, on the edge.
Our relationships with our colleagues, that perhaps at another
time could have been solidary, today are tarnished with savage
competition: for contemporary capitalism, an individual is their
own company, and companies do not have colleagues but com-
petitors. Precarity encompasses all of this. In this context (and
this is where I deviate from Lorey's original idea although, I
believe, without betraying it), is it not logical that we look for
"something stable" to hold on to? Something that is "mine and
mine only" and that no one can steal from me, take away, turn
precarious? Is it not understandable that we continue to introduce and persevere with relationships that are restrictive and
unequal, that we continue to think that this sacrifice is "worth
it" like citizens who accept an increase in police controls because they prefer that to the threat of insecurity? Just like those
citizens, we are all confused if we choose monogamy for that
reason. There is no bond that can save us from the precarious condition of our lives and of human relationships. A signed
piece of paper or a love promise are not enough to hide the fact
that everything can break at any moment (the generation of our
parents knows this all too well!). There is no way out of it. The
peace that we dream of, that illusion of security, is a fantasy we
need to let go of because, just like the police state, it comes with
its own precarity.

I don't know how old Pablo is. I never saw him in person,
and I only heard stories of him. I asked my ex-boyfriend to
share his email address with me because I remembered those
stories. Pablo is a friend of my ex's mother, Silvina, and he's famous in the family circle for having maintained a three-person

relationship for many years. I'm interested in his case because, although I'm not sure of his age, it's similar to Silvina's, so he must be around sixty. I hate confirming other people's prejudices, but as my friends and I approach thirty, a lot of what we were told would happen is indeed happening. People who used to disparage monogamy now upload pictures with their marriage certificate and rice falling on them like microprojectiles at the registry office; others who promised they would never have children and would spend their lives travelling around the world are having children and are not travelling around the world. As I sense that many who are experimenting with poly-amory today might give it up in the next decade, I was interested in talking with someone whose search lies outside of the mononormative[22] and has transcended the explorative years of youth. This is why I decided to write to Pablo without a clear list of questions. Just to talk, so he could tell me whatever he wished, whatever he thought might be interesting.

"I have had many long-term relationships: one from when I was twenty-four to twenty-eight, another one from the age of twenty-eight to forty, and my current one that began as a three-way relationship when I was forty-nine and continues happily despite the break-up with one of them two years ago," writes Pablo from Spain, where he has been living for some time. "I had different 'formulas' one after the other: permitting each other to be involved in other situations but discussing them openly, permitting each other to be involved in other situations but keeping them hidden, permitting each other to be involved in other situations but always including the other partner (this is easier and more common within the gay community), or not permitting each other to do any of these things. I have also seen these formulas be used by other couples. There's an assumption that, behind these formulas and the corresponding option chosen by a person or a couple, there is an ethical and moral way of being and behaving. You seek out and discuss what the concepts of fidelity and loyalty mean. However, from my point of view, in general we try to adapt reality to our own system rather than the other way around, and this is always a problem that ends up generating conflict."

Pablo and Luis had been living together for many years; one night they went out ("on the pull" as Pablo says) after some time of not looking outside of their relationship, and they met Pedro, a very handsome man twenty years younger. They invited him to their house. "I can assure you that this was a love story from the beginning, but it wasn't focused on sex. The sexual side of things didn't work so well between the three of us," he tells me. After a couple of weeks, Pedro moved in with them indefinitely and the three of them formed a family that, despite a lot of tension, lasted ten and a half years. At that point, Pablo and Pedro realized that they wanted to continue being together but that they had distanced themselves from Luis, which is what they said to him. "And no, Tamara, I do not want to have anything to do with three-way relationships," he responds to my question of whether they would try to be together again. "Never in my life have I been as happy as I am now. And, yes, since we have been 'alone,' Pedro and I have learned to love each other in every sense of the word, including of course sexually (which is so meaningful). This process has been and is fabulous: being with someone you have shared a life with for ten years but in a new way—a new house, new neighborhood, a new way of cohabiting, new sex, new horizons. It was a vital injection in my sixties. A wonderful new outlook. A very brave jump, with all the risks such a jump entails. Something many people in our lives could not or did not want to comprehend because, at my age Tamara, most people are on the conservative path, in their comfort zones, and in a way, the path that leads to death. And this caused great upset amid that fragile happiness. Even if I know that 'what others think does not matter.' But we have also overcome that now. When you break something that's so important, in reality, you're breaking much more than the obvious, you cut off other things, people, places, And such is life. It doesn't come with a manual of instructions, the opposite in fact." That's the phrase Pablo used to conclude his first email.

I had already read in Deborah Anapol's book that we should not fetishize the *ways* in which we relate to others, that what is important is not the number of participants in a relationship but the principles, the values, and affections that said relationship is based on. But frankly, I thought that was a consolation prize for those who, like I did, read that book from our monogamous situations, and felt guilty of not deconstructing enough to experience what she discussed. Talking to Pablo I understood the true meaning of this interpretation. For him—in his world, at his age, and with his personal history—, "daring to want more" meant turning his three-way relationship into a couple without letting routine rule, without allowing the expectations of friends or theoretical duties relating sexual freedom govern him.

I asked him what he meant by "adapt reality to our own system rather than the other way around, and this is always a problem that ends up generating conflict." "This example illustrates the meaning I wanted to convey with that phrase: when it comes to agreeing with our partner on the conditions of fidelity, we can demand more than what we are prepared to offer, but the opposite can also be the case. Before agreeing, we can bridge the gap between our personal situation and our partner's situation, hence becoming more sympathetic and having a better view of ourselves. However, any agreement based on these terms—which are extremely normal—will inevitably lead to conflict as we have happily reached an agreement, but we have lied to ourselves," he explains. "All the formulas of fidelity within a couple are deficient at a certain point, but I believe there is a solution, which is by no means definitive and stems from our own experiences and from honesty. I know myself;

I know what I want, and I negotiate to acquire it." His words remind me of what Gino and Bárbara told me about their failed attempts to negotiate open relationships with people who did not want them. How flexible is desire? Is it possible to deconstruct "ad infinitum" or is there a limit that can only be crossed with the body? "We cannot ask for more flexibility nor offer it when it is simply not possible," says Pablo, in a tautological yet very truthful phrase. "Nor are there any formulas for this. Although I am certain of something—as always due to my own experience—love always manages to break through innumerable sexual barriers."

I ask myself about my own barriers. Sometimes I believe I would love to live a polyamorous life, continually searching and exploring others' touch. But in general, I feel that I am not cut out for it, that I am too tired and that all the instability I can tolerate is covered by trying to make a living out of writing. Perhaps in the future I will feel differently. I suppose we all have a limit. Bárbara and Gino are sexually open but exclusive when it comes to affection. They feel that anything different would be an investment of energy and time that they would not know how to manage. I feel the same way about the constant sexual experimentation they speak of. I understand that for them sexuality is not only a portion of their lives but rather a path of genuine exploration, and even a space of creation and self-awareness. I don't know if I'll ever be able to develop that relationship with my own sexuality. At times I ask myself if, just like other people choose yoga, dancing, or poetry as a privileged space of exploration, there are those who choose sex almost as a vocation. And perhaps that is not my case. My sexuality is important to me, but not in that way.

I don't know if polyamorous relationships bring more happiness than monogamous ones, but I have realized one thing: in the same way that I intuited an oddity about everyone dressing in the same way when I was a child, those who walk away from what is expected of them are more likely to prioritize desire and their happiness above all conventions, and that is a good path to follow. It seems to me that it's no coincidence that the vast majority of people I know, who are not involved in traditional relationships, are part of the queer community: those who neither can nor want to comply with the heteronormative mandate take a leap in the venture of betting on desire. I believe this is what feminist bell hooks refers to when she says that marginality is a space of resistance from which it is possible to build a radical perspective on society.[23] In a way, that space between the inside and the outside of society represents an epistemic position of privilege—those who are left outside of the norm can see, experiment, and name things that those who are inside it fail to see. I want to learn more about that leap, that pull, and that possibility of giving life to questions that sting.

I also think about my broken barriers, about my successes. I believe that the most important one is one that Anapol discusses in her book as the difference between relationships following the old paradigm and those following the new paradigm. Without making value judgements, Anapol proposes that a couple in the old paradigm can be open or exclusive, but what defines it is the hierarchy of the bond between the two parties above the other bonds they each have; following the new paradigm, on the other hand, it is understood that the couple (which could even have a different name or include more than two people) is for each of the members an insertion into a larger community, one more bond in a constellation of loving relationships (familial, friendships, sexual, emotional, or any others that are desired). I don't believe my relationship fully falls under the "new paradigm," but I do work hard to make it so. When I was a teenager, I could have cancelled plans with any of my friends to go out for a meal with my boyfriend, and this would have been an acceptable decision. Now, although I live with my boyfriend, my friends often stay over, they are a part of our home and our daily lives. We share food shops with them, and they have keys to the house. They know things about me that he does not, and there are certain things I prefer to discuss with them instead of him. When I imagine my old age, I picture it with them. None of these things, I believe, are manifestations of a threat to the romantic bond, and he has a similar relationship with many friends of both genders. I feel similarly towards my passion, writing. Whole weeks go by when my boyfriend and I each mind our own business because I need to concentrate all my energy on a project that I am working on, which demands it and absorbs me completely. I'm not going to say that the couple does not suffer following those periods of isolation because it's not true; I often suffer greatly. But it's true that, pain and all, we try to respect those needs and not question what is more important or what should be more important (or at least we try not to do it too frequently).

My boyfriend and I have something else in common, which to me is a great achievement, we both have an ex we care deeply about and whom we speak to frequently. This may seem like a minor detail, but I believe that the capacity to transform bonds instead of discarding them is a crucial learning that defies old prejudices about what we are supposed to feel towards our previous lovers and our partner's previous lovers. I first thought of the relevance of this when I read Judith Butler, in her dialogue with Athena Athanasiou, *Dispossession: The Performative in the Political*,[24] where she explains an aspect that can be present in many friendship groups within the LGBTQI+ community: relationships between former lovers can be and often are the pillars of a queer friendship. The end of romantic love does not necessarily mean, as has been historically considered, the end of love. And this is crucial as it relates to a departure from the logic of individualism and takes community as an entity to be analyzed, as a referent, and as a transformative horizon. If queer people choose not to disappear from the life of their former partner when the sexual relationship ends, it is also because they have a notion of belonging and of the collective, they know that they must look after each other, that they are always in danger: "regardless of who you are sleeping with, we must look after each other."

This is what I understand as the new paradigm. Betting on friendships as common policy, the construction of consensual and serious (meaning important) emotional bonds which still relish a certain flexibility, are characterized by responsibility but also by understanding, and that can either be sexual or not. Building communities of love and friendship as solid support systems while accepting the precarious condition of existence and relationships. There is only one way out of that curious mix of dependence and solipsism that we find ourselves in because of the contemporary emphasis placed on the couple, and that is an explosion of affection. The couple can only be saved if we decenter it, if we remove it from the podium of life, if we cease to think of it as the finish line in the race of love, as the result of or the ultimate expression of love. And, more importantly, because crucially, I don't care about saving the couple: with great love, friendships, communities, and luck perhaps we can at least manage to save ourselves.

# CHAPTER 4
## THE MARKET OF DESIRE

Thinking of contemporary couples frustrates me in two different ways. Firstly, the most complicated part lies in overcoming old traditions by recognizing the extent to which women are still governed by norms that subordinate us politically, socially, and financially; and removing ourselves from the situations characterized by domination that we often feed into and reinforce because we never had the time, space, nor money to learn to do otherwise. Secondly, I am frustrated by more recent problems. Those that arrived with new technologies and that increasingly affect the way in which our identities are built within the market, and the ways in which aspiration and consumerism invade every corner of our lives, even those we (think we) strive to keep outside of the sphere of calculation. Both conflicts seem to me interesting and important. In the context of the couple, I am more concerned with what hasn't changed than what has, because in reality, I don't believe very much has.

When it comes to singlehood, the contrary has happened instead. In the last fifty or sixty years, everything has changed. We could almost say that there is no benchmark, as what we call singlehood today didn't exist a couple of generations ago. It still doesn't exist in Orthodox Once and perhaps it never will. If it did, Once would no longer be Once. There, most women marry between the ages of eighteen and twenty-two, in some ultraorthodox families it can happen even earlier, but in modern Orthodox Argentina, girls are expected to finish high school and then begin forming a family. The search for a husband, however, normally begins during the last years of school. From the age of fifteen or sixteen, it's common to see girls straightening their hair, wearing more expensive or striking clothing (within the parameters of the Tzniut or "modesty"), and even losing weight. Finding a husband is essential and the pressure of finding a "good one" (a boy from a recognized family, relatively young, and in a good financial position) is high because girls' financial and social prospects depend on it. And it better happen early, as after the age of twenty-three, twenty-four, and twenty-five you are competing with "newcomers" who are eighteen and nineteen years old, and your chances of forming a suitable marriage (or any marriage at all) fall exponentially.

But whether that post-adolescent period of "no marriage" lasts one, ten, or fifty years, it can hardly be compared with singlehood in the secular world. Couples have barely changed, as I've said several times. Our ideas of fidelity are very similar to those held by our parents, even though we're not fully comfortable with them and despite the fact that an increasing number of people dare to think of different emotional agreements. However, the way in which we live outside of the couple has completely transformed. Unmarried girls from Once largely stay at their family homes. If they're lucky, they have a room of their own, though more often they share it with their sisters, regardless of their age, but sleep in their individual beds. Many of them work (as teachers or secretaries in a community center or the family business), but they would never dream of abandoning the family home and, although they bring income for the family, they are treated as if they were eternal adolescents.[1]

I recently read an article in *The New York Times*[2] that told the story of a group of girls belonging to the Modern Orthodox community, the same one I come from, who lived together. This struck me as peculiar since I don't know of many cases like that. I found it amusing that the article conveyed a clear curiosity about the girls' shared living situation and about how different their apartment was to any other household of single women—and not only because they cooked Kosher food and had rules about not using the computer in the sitting room during Shabbat, but because they slept in the same rooms. Two girls shared a room and slept in twin beds, even though they were all over thirty years old. Throughout the article the journalist avoids the elephant in the room: the reason they sleep together is not because they believe in sharing, in the feminine, in communal living; the reason they sleep together is because they don't have sex with anyone.

In the twenty-first century, for most of us being single means having sex with lots of different people: simultaneously or in succession, continually or sporadically. Having sex with friends, with friends of friends, with people we met in a bar or on the internet, with ex partners, with someone who might become our partner in the future (which happens infrequently), with people who are in other relationships—open or exclusive—in summary, with anyone. This was not always the case (for women). It's a recent phenomenon that has been accepted socially even more recently.

In her book *Future Sex*, writer Emily Witt begins by considering the significance of the contemporary state of relationships and how we rarely recognize its historical value. She suggests that, in fact, the way we relate to each other in this case is such a novelty that language has not advanced enough to be able to keep up with its pace. There are no exact words to describe relationships we have when we're not *in* a relationship.[3] She continues to name various options in English (hooking up, lovers, or dating), which are quite inadequate. In *Rioplatense* Spanish we have the same problem: the phrase "I am going out with someone" is very ambiguous. It can refer to a boyfriend of many years, to someone we've met up with a couple of times, or to someone we've been messaging for months and have sex with every now and then. The term "*chonguear*" [which could be translated as "situationship"] has a more informal connotation and is equally imprecise. I know a girl who is the epitome of elegance and simply calls people she's seeing *friends*, but that doesn't solve the issue of ambiguity either.

Witt doesn't consider this lack of precise terms for talking about these types of bonds to be a coincidence nor a matter of time. In a society in which the couple continues to be the target when it comes to female happiness, those who are not in a couple don't want to allude to their situation. We want to think, writes Witt, that this is a temporary situation, an "interim" while we wait for that love that will arrive for all of us as a given right or as a natural blessing. Is being single always a choice? asks Witt playfully and repeatedly throughout her book. This is a more complicated question to answer than it may appear. Unless someone has offered to be your partner and you have refused, in general, being single is the result of cumulative choices and coincidences: perhaps you haven't crossed paths with a person worth forming a relationship with or with a person who wants to form one with you, but most likely there have been people you could have started a relationship with and you chose not to.

The concept of the proud single woman who goes out every night and always has a good time doesn't encompass the variety of ways in which singlehood is experienced in the twenty-first century. If we welcome the label of proud single woman, it's because it allows us to move away from two concepts that we fear more than we fear the consumerist banality of the "girls' nights out"—characteristic of fake empowerment and discounts for girls-only tables—: the "spinster" on the one hand and the "desperate woman" on the other hand. The proud single woman keeps her desires in check (unlike the desperate woman, who desires and shows her desires to an extent much greater than that which the patriarchy considers dignified) and is single because she wants to be (unlike the spinster, a frigid woman who is not the object of desire of any man and, hence, is of no value). The concept of proud single women is ideal for the patriarchy because this woman desires just enough not to question anything. She doesn't believe there's anything wrong with the way contemporary sexual and emotional relationships are processed: bad behavior, ignorance, indifference, and even violence, are all fun or at least "will serve as a good anecdote." She doesn't cry like the desperate woman who complains that there are "no men," nor does she pose a threat like the spinster, who doesn't seem to need men.

Most women don't fall under any of these archetypes, but at different stages they might relate to one or all of them, to a different extent. But, aside from social and personal perceptions, we cannot deny that in the third millennium singlehood is a reality that we all experience and that we all come back to. In the neighborhood where I grew up, where divorce is reserved only for very few cases, women are either married or single. In the rest of the city, conversely, people come in and out of couple life almost as often as they walk in and out of their houses.

This has been the case for at least two decades. Among my friends from high school, which I attended from 2002 until 2006, only two out of thirty-six students had parents who were still married or would stay married throughout those years. However, we still believe singlehood to be a transitional period, something that happens between "forming bonds" rather than a particular way of forming bonds. Just like in romantic comedies, we believe singlehood to be the kind of standstill that Witt talks about. It's those twenty minutes it takes a heroine to bump into her prince charming on the street, or those episodes halfway through a season when she speaks to her friends about how awful a time she's having. It's a narrative tension that at one point *must* be resolved. "You will find someone eventually," the women who are in a relationship say to their single friends, with a combination of hope and condescension (we must admit that, even in the secular world, women who are in monogamous relationships still talk to single women as if they were younger than them, as if the ones who are married had won the race of life and the rest are still miles behind). I deliberately rather than incidentally speak only of women. Being in a relationship or not is a criterion to classify women rather than people. Women, and particularly heterosexual women, are the ones who are socially defined by our relationship with a man (whom we belong to) or all men we could potentially belong to (because if we aren't "taken" we are public property). This is how the heteronormative point of view labels us, as "taken" or "available." It's not without reason that in most languages, a woman goes from "Miss" to "Mrs." when she marries, but a man is a "Mr." in both cases.

The narrative that attempts to stop the bad press around singlehood by calling it "fun" or "an opportunity to get to know yourself" is part of the problem rather than the solution. In the same way the call to "love yourself as you are" cohabits with unattainable beauty standards, this narrative highlights the question of individual attitude (and as a result, the question of a supposed responsibility women have for not being able to love themselves enough). By doing so, it deviates the attention from the real reasons why, in many women's experience, singlehood doesn't work. It's not in your head, it's not bad luck, it's not happening only to you: the market of desire, as Eva Illouz calls it,[4] is a historical reality moved by powers that are beyond you.

When I began writing the agony aunt column "for the digital generation" at the newspaper I work for, I received very few letters. I even had to resort to asking my friends to write in or making up issues myself. Now, almost two years after starting the column, I receive between five and fifteen emails each week and have to select which ones to answer. Still, it's difficult to find a good story every week. Ninety percent of the emails are the same. I've even come up with three different versions addressing issues such as "he doesn't answer my messages but looks at all my Instagram stories," "how to put a stop to WhatsApp hysteria," or "it takes fourteen hours for him to reply to my messages, is it because he doesn't like me?" Every now and then different issues come up, but there's a striking likeness between the topics these girls write to me about. Another recurring coincidence is their age: at least from what I'm reading, these things happen mostly to women under the age of thirty-five. Other than that, the crowd is greatly diverse—university students, housewives, call center workers, secretaries, lawyers. Women who work from the crack of dawn until sunset, others who have been married and divorced, some who had children when they were teenagers or who study full time at an expensive private university. An entire sisterhood agonizingly waiting by the phone.

Almost all these women begin their emails by downplaying the discomfort that motivated them to write to me: "I know this is stupid and I shouldn't worry so much about him," in different words depending on their style, "*but* the truth is that I'm very upset, and I don't know what to do." I get a feeling that there's something relatively new in that apology, a generational cue: we understand that being modern and self-affirmed women means not being focused on men, but we understand this in a rather curious way. We know that it means not becoming attached, not feeling judged by the way they treat us, and not demanding anything they don't want to give us—even if it's a minor gesture or a glass of water. Adapting to their desires and making it seem like pure chance without asking for more or giving any less. In three words, not pestering them.

Once when I was twenty or twenty-one years old, at around 10 P.M. I went to the house of a man I had been sleeping with sporadically. I didn't expect candles or even a set table, but I asked him if he had anything in the fridge because I had come straight from university and hadn't eaten. "I didn't bring you here to eat," he answered, annoyed. Initially, I thought he was joking, but he didn't offer me anything. I simply smiled and lay on his bed. He didn't invite me to his kitchen even after we had sex. I only ever saw his kitchen because one entered the apartment he shared with a friend through there, followed by the hallway, and his bedroom. I never walked around the apartment, not even to see what the living room was like or to change station on the radio: he would have deemed that a total intrusion, signaling a level of trust that—as he and many other men I have been with presumed—could lead a woman to concoct "strange ideas" about the future of the bond we shared. I understood and accepted this. Because I didn't want him to think that I would fall in love with him and that I was a weight on his shoulders, I never questioned those limits. In general, we had a good time, but was all that necessary? Would a slice of cheese and some crackers have implied too much of a commitment? Of course, I acknowledge the part I had to play. Why did I not say anything? Why did I not insist and tell him that I was truly hungry? Why did I not laugh it off and walk to the fridge?

Gillian Flynn describes this very well in her novel *Gone Girl*, in a monologue that all my friends shared on Facebook when the movie adaptation was released: "Being the *Cool Girl* means I am a hot, brilliant, funny woman who adores football, poker, dirty jokes, and burping, who plays video games, drinks cheap beer, loves threesomes and anal sex, and jams hot dogs and hamburgers into her mouth like she's hosting the world's biggest culinary gang bang while somehow maintaining a size 2, because *Cool Girls* are above all hot. Hot and understanding. Cool Girls never get angry; they only smile in a chagrined, loving manner and let their men do whatever they want. Go ahead, shit on me, I don't mind, I'm the *Cool Girl*."[5]

Flynn's description contains many cultural particularities that vary according to their context, but she highlights a key transformation in the dynamics of heterosexual singlehood that took place in recent years and that I am interested in highlighting. Women who have sex are no longer a nuisance, although there is still no room in society for female desire. Being "easy" is no longer an issue, it stopped being an issue when I was younger. On the contrary, we all want that image: being easy means not causing problems, reaching orgasm through penetration, and always at the right moment. But desire doesn't work that way, desire cannot be perfectly symmetrical every time, I would even go as far as to say that it never is. It is part of the shock force, constant discoordination, hence when sparks fly in an encounter with another, they are explosive—because they are uncommon, scarce, because they are always insufficient. In that insufficiency lies the power that allows for the search to continue inexhaustibly. If we limit ourselves to adapting to what men seem to want and attempt to guess what they desire, our own desire is left buried in oblivion and theirs is too in a sense. Without resistance, without any demand coming from the other side, without a subject with a personal identity, having sex with someone is synonymous with masturbating with an inflatable doll. It does not surprise me that myriad women go years without having an orgasm, that myriad women have never received cunnilingus from a man or ever even thought of asking for it. We learn to satisfy our pleasure by pleasing the other. It is a hugely important part of sex (half of it, perhaps), but it cannot be all of it. In that struggle to not do anything strange, to not ask, to not become a nuisance, your body begins to turn into a tool not only for others but also for yourself: something that is *useful*, that you make use of, but do not experience. You begin to separate from it, you begin a dissociation. Still, that's preferable to being perceived as difficult—a demanding girl who gets angry, who says yes to this but no to that, who says "that hurts" or "I like that." And this is not only applied to sex because, of course, desire is not only related to sex.

The Cool Girl creed that my generation learned isn't about the specific desires of certain men; it doesn't relate, as it once did, to a husband explicitly controlling his wife, even if that still occurs, albeit not as the norm. The Cool Girl is historically tied to the idea of a submissive woman who endures it all, even violence, but it doesn't originate there exclusively. It is also an effect of the emergence of the market logic in the sexual and emotional sphere, driven by the need to always increase your value not by being the one who satisfies her own pleasure but rather by being the coolest: never too crazy, always being "chill." It is the same logic that implies that we deal with encounters with others as transactional periods from which we take only what is useful and avoid preoccupying ourselves with the harm caused along the way because we can always justify it by saying: "it's not my responsibility because we're not boyfriend and girl-friend, or anything like that." It's not singlehood, dear friend, that hurts; it's not casual sex, the fluidity of our bonds, nor their ephemeral nature that causes pain: it's the dynamic of supply and demand, which, just as in the market of goods and services, is heading in one clear direction.

In the neighborhood where I was born, the process of choos-ing a partner is much more ritualized and, above all, less indi-vidualistic than in the secular world. In Once, things are more informal: couples can be formed after both parties cross paths in the synagogue or simply because someone's nephew or an adult they both know thinks it's a good idea. In the Orthodox Jewish communities of the United Stated, on the other hand, there are professional matchmakers who are paid for their work. They re-ceive printed CVs to form suitable pairings. The path that leads to people finding each other is neither chaotic nor rhizomatic; it rather resembles centralized planning of a Soviet nature by having someone distributing "romantic resources" according to criteria deemed valid by the collective. The willingness of both parties involved in the arrangements is minor, if not irrelevant. Romantic relationships are embedded in the social and economic structure of society, and the values that guide it are collective and shared rather than individual and personal.

Eva Illouz became famous throughout the world by explaining how this overlap of structures is deconstructed in contemporary societies. She takes this concept from economist Karl Polanyi, who explains how in capitalism, the economy is detached from society and of normative or ethical framings so that it can be autonomous in self-regulated markets, and continue to subsume all the spheres of society under its regulations. "What we call the 'triumph' of romantic love in relations between the sexes," writes Illouz, "consisted first and foremost in the dis-embedding of individual romantic choices from the moral and social fabric of the group and in the emergence of a self-regulated market of encounters. Modern criteria to evaluate a love object have become disentangled from publicly shared moral frameworks. This disentanglement occurred because of a transformation of the content of the criteria for selecting a mate—which have become both physical/sexual and emotional/psychological—and because of a transformation of the very process of mate selection—which has become both more subjective and more individualized."[6]

The phrase "market of desire" is not simply a disparaging term, but a concept that helps explain the way in which the sexual and emotional relationships we build today—seemingly free and individualistic—respond to the reality of the logic of the market, of decentralization and disorganization. It can sound cold and dehumanizing, but what is interesting about this concept is thinking about the extent to which the way we behave in trade transactions can be applied to our understanding of erotic encounters.

When a person buys a shirt, part of that transaction can be considered personal and individual: they choose to buy that specific shirt and not another, in that moment, in that place, of that color, because they want to. We understand this, but that does not mean that what conditions that exchange is less valid or less visible. This individual buys a shirt that they can afford of a size that fits them and is available from a place they have access to, in the color that's in fashion that season because a magazine said so; they bought it because they think they need a shirt (perhaps they do "need" it, no one is denying this) or because they enjoy shopping for clothes. We all like the clothes we like but those preferences are not always random. There are organizations or groups that have the power to set trends, there are aspirations and beauty standards, there are intersubjective parameters, and there are cost variations that generally reflect some kind of hidden hierarchy. Social impositions intertwine in a seemingly individual, banal, and free action. If political economy involves restoring those underlying relations of trade transactions, applying political economy to love requires we do the same with our bonds: showing that behind that apparent chaos there might not be an order (in a sense, the most pronounced characteristic of our times is chaos) but instead operating powers, asymmetry, and recurring dynamics. In other words, going from "why do these things always happen to me?" to "why do these things happen to so many of us?"

Illouz does not speak of Instagram stories nor of read receipts on WhatsApp, she speaks of several phenomena that are a couple of decades older and that are the foundations of many situations we go through in the present time (no, the internet is not the only one to blame). The uncertainty that characterizes all our erotic encounters today, for example, is rooted in this process of deconstructing the rituals that appear in love in the twentieth century, in particular since the sixties. This isn't to say that before then, and in communities that still function with dated rules, things were certain: anyone who has read Jane Austen knows this isn't true. But those courtship rules *protected* women to a certain extent (to not say restricted them) from the volatility of the other's desire. Breaking up a commitment or pursuing a woman without asking for her hand in marriage was greatly frowned upon (we see it in *Sense and Sensibility* with Willoughby for example), attributing a detrimental nature to these behaviors not only for the woman in question, but also for the man, who risked his reputation as an honorable, righteous man. These standardized rituals also prevented misunderstandings. A visit, a present, two dances in a row; all these events had a clear and commonly understood meaning. It is fortunate that things worked this way because the issue of whether to marry or not and who with was a matter of life or death for young women of that time. Their subsistence depended on it, their possibility of having a sexual life and of giving their lives the only meaning that was available for them.

The contrast between their universe and ours could not be greater. On the bus, on the streets, at the bar in a nightclub, at tables in a bar, my university students and the girls who write to me all ask themselves the same question: "what did he mean?" My friends and I have fortunately grown tired of the subject (or we have learned to decodify it more easily), but up until a few years ago, we still sent each other pages-long conversations we had had with the boys we liked to be interpreted in the group chat.

It's not only the words we exchange which are full of opaque and manifold meanings; actions or invitations do not imply the same in all the cases either. This, says Eva Illouz, is one of the most important achievements of the sexual revolution: having sex with someone no longer carries underlying meaning and is neither good nor bad. It doesn't presume a commitment or a bond, although it doesn't exclude the possibility of one. A night of good sex can be the beginning of something—it can mark the start of a sporadic bond or a stable one, perhaps even a friendly one (this might be my favorite outcome)—or it can simply end at that. We never know, unless the other decides to be explicit (an extremely rare occurrence). There are no longer common social canons denoting the necessary and adequate conditions for a commitment. It is also no longer presumed that we are all looking to form a relationship or to commit in any way and at any time in our lives.

Many of our daily misfortunes are not only inevitable but also occasionally blessings in disguise. Freedom always entails disappointment and risk; we can no longer pretend to be protected against rejection, unrequited love, loss of love, indifference, or being hurt. The risk of being hurt is a constituent element of love. Without vulnerability, without the tangible possibility of damage, there is no real opening up to another person. However, I cannot help feeling uncomfortable about one thing: There's no denying that men too get their hearts broken, but in most stories that go nowhere, that revolve around apathy and disinterest, women are the ones who suffer most. They are the ones who wait by the telephone, the ones who calculate how many hours it's been since they saw their message, the ones who ask themselves why they haven't replied, the ones who collectively debate conjectures and strategies with their friends. Why is it that often in the heterosexual world men seem to be the ones who continuously and unilaterally set the terms? And why do women so often seem to wait hopefully for an idiot they aren't truly interested in? I'm aware that this sounds like a stereotype and that we tend to reject any characterization akin to a romantic comedy based on relationships and gender roles, and rightly so as neither all women want to fall in love, nor all men escape relationships. But a great number of women relate to this description and ask themselves why they cannot "manage" to make a man fall in love with them, why all men ignore their messages, why all men disappear, why all men seem cold, why they don't care how it feels when they stop answering calls. That distress is real and to underestimate it with "please, stop being such a chaser!" or "you can't let your life revolve around trying to get in some guy's pants!" would not be a response characteristic of sorority:[7] thinking that women or feminists are "beyond" these triggers of distress generates the dissociation the girls who write to my agony aunt column speak of—those girls who suffer and simultaneously feel guilt for allowing issues that are too trivial for the cool girls they pretend to be affect them.

Disparaging this feeling is not only a response lacking in sorority, but it is also a missed opportunity when it comes to understanding how the correlation between the powers behind the emotional market operate and how they produce and reinforce certain practices and subjectivities. In the third chapter of *Why Love Hurts*, Eva Illouz analyzes this phenomenon she calls male detachment. Collectively shared theories about men's emotional inaptitude, she explains, do not add to sociological analysis not because they might not be true, but because they come from values that believe commitment to be the parameter of what is right, hence presuming that those who reject it are at fault. Illouz is interested in analyzing whether the current way in which we organize our erotic decisions makes so many men behave this way in relationships. And the answer is yes: many factors converge to allow emotional and sexual detachment to become a prevalent strategy among men.

In the societies of the West, says Illouz, quoting historian John Tosh, masculinity is manifested in three spheres: the home, the workplace, and exclusively male institutions (this could range from a private members' club to a football game). Throughout the twentieth century, however, male authority in the home and in the workplace diminished, partly because of the feminist revolution and partly due to the mass growth of wage labor, which resulted in most of the workforce not exerting authority in the workplace but rather answering to authority. Simultaneously, spaces with gender segregation began to disappear or to lose importance (with the clear exception of sporting events).

Illouz's thesis then explains that masculinity—understood as a particular combination of autonomy, authority, and intra-gender solidarity—is today manifested in the sexual sphere and, to a lesser extent (or at least not more than before) through violence. It manifests in the small yet significant power of indifference. "Men transferred to sex and sexuality the control they had formerly held in the household, and sexuality became the realm within which they could express and display their authority and their autonomy. Detachment in sexuality came to signal and organize the broader trope of autonomy and control, and, thus, of masculinity. Emotional detachment could be viewed as a metaphor for masculine autonomy."[8]

Of course, the correlation between sexuality and power, or rather between male power and the access to multiple sexual partners, is not new. However, in the early twentieth century, that opportunity was exclusive to powerful men (kings, aristocrats, officers of the army). Today, there are many more men who can form a personal harem. But they must remain indifferent to achieve that, never risk becoming *trapped* by a woman or allow her to decide if the relationship will progress or not. She must be the one who waits, who reacts, who adapts. The women who protest against this asymmetry, who demand, who clearly explain what they want instead of following the rules of the game laid out by the man, will not face violence or discipline, they will be ignored. Illouz interviewed a group of men of various ages and there was a recurring theme: "the desperate woman" or the idea that a woman who wants compromise instantly becomes less attractive. This partly has to do with the dynamic of desire of course. All women and all men want, to some extent, what they don't have, what they're missing. But again, there is asymmetry here: men insist that longing for commitment obliterates sexual desire, while women rarely support that argument.

Why does this strategy work for men? Why do women not only not tire of the indifferent ones, but persevere? Illouz's answers are unpleasant, particularly for those of us who often forget that deconstruction is not a path with a beginning and an ending but an outlook on life that is inconclusive. For heterosexual cis women, maternity, in the traditional sense of the word (biological and in the context of a monogamous relationship), continues to be a decisive factor to aspire to; even those of us who are still unsure when reaching a certain age, begin to feel as though we should *create the right conditions* to have children *just in case*, to not regret it *when it is too late*. There are two advantages to being a man in this respect: on the one hand, men's fertility declines much more slowly—and this information is widely understood and hence functional—and, on the other hand and perhaps more importantly, in our society a man is not defined by whether or not he has children. No one believes that the life of a man without children is empty or that he is *lacking* in any way. However, this point of view is still extremely common when applied to women. And I'm not only referring to the stigma faced by those who choose not to have children, but also those who perhaps had maternal desires which did not manifest for reasons unrelated to their choosing (to become a mother, it must be said, desire alone is not sufficient). The fear of becoming one of these women whom society views as outcasts (even though they may not necessarily be unhappier; plenty of studies show there is no direct correlation between having children and happiness)[9] is powerful. It generates subjectivity and dynamics that we often struggle to see from the outside; the fear of becoming a crazy cat lady is—as is the fear of being raped—a form of discipline that we internalize without question.

As if this was not enough, the worship of youth and beauty, particularly when imposed on women, makes us feel that leading a sexual or emotional life is almost impossible once we are past a certain "expiry date." In a recent study published by the magazine *Science Advances*,[10] this difference is evidenced with an astonishing preciseness: according to the data from a "free and extremely popular dating app," men's desirability peaks at fifty years old. Women's, however, starts very high at eighteen years old and decreases with time. The exact numbers might be new to us, but in general terms, the majority of women already knew this; whether consciously or not, many of our desires, fears, and behaviors are based on this information.

Until the twentieth century, both men and women had plenty of motivations to invest in a stable relationship. Today, although there are still those who continue to benefit from women's unpaid labor (Illouz shows this paradox in her book: men gain a lot more from marriage than women, according to the available evidence),[11] there are still socially available incentives for a man to not need to build a family in order to "become a man" in the terms that society proposes: professional success and a sufficient number of sexual partners are a lot closer to male aspirations than the choice to become a father or not. On the other hand, in order to "become a woman" in hegemonic terms, having biological children in the context of a stable relationship continues to be a *sine qua non* condition. I often remember the case of Paloma Herrera, one of the best ballerinas of her generation internationally. It was only after the *Ni Una Menos* (Not one woman less) movement, when we began to talk more fervently about what feminist journalism meant, that I was able to find interviews in which she was not referred to as a poor childless woman.

Because of these factors, women today not only bear the

responsibility of nurturing relationships and families but also of desiring them. In *Labor of Love*, Moira Weigel[12] returns to the concept of emotional labor coined by sociologist Arlie Rusell Hochschild to explain that for women the world of dating works not only as a market, as Illouz had already proposed, but also as a labor market. From a young age, we learn to apply for the position and begin to consider which are the valued virtues to be highlighted (being the Cool Girl would be the equivalent of "being proactive" at work) and which are the shortcomings to be overcome. I remember vividly the moment when I first realized, on a third date with a boy when I was fifteen years old, that showing my interest the first or second time was acceptable, but after that it had to be exhibited in small instalments so that his desire would not wane. Just as we learned that working is mandatory for most of us, we also learn that this side job is also mandatory; that although we no longer need to practice celibacy nor stay pure until marriage—we can go out with whomever we want—we must not lose sight of the end goal and of the countdown. And this is not only exhausting and alienating, like most jobs, it's also an extremely dull way of having sex and loving.

I've been trying to have conversations on these topics with my friends recently. I have a personal vendetta against "rejection culture" when it comes to gender stereotypes: the idea that if we repeatedly tell ourselves that this is all a lie—that the symbolic engine of the biological clock isn't restricting us, that we aren't like those ridiculous women who cry by the telephone in soap operas—then this narrative will disintegrate as if by magic. I'm not moved by the false empowerment of motivational phrases. I prefer to try to understand that we're all learning, that we still don't know which are the alternatives to the paradigms we've inherited and continue repeating, and that perhaps we might never know.

However, I do believe that many of these issues are changing and not in the way previous generations thought they would. The famous "new masculinity" for example—men who feel oppressed rather than liberated by the demand to exert authority through detachment—is one of the unsuspected novelties I've been noticing among men of my generation and the one after. Men who were upset about the erratic behavior of a girl began to write to my agony aunt column. This is what a centennial wrote to me:

> I met a girl who drives me crazy. After a few days of chatting over WhatsApp, we arranged to meet up and I thought it had gone very well. She seemed willing to try things out with me. We kissed and had a great day together. Everything was going well, the good-byes were amazing, I could tell that she liked me, and she even said that she didn't want me to lie to her, and that I should be honest with her about everything.
>
> I was hopeful because I could see that she was getting attached already. However, that same evening, speaking over WhatsApp, I noticed that she was behaving strangely. She began to try to make me feel jealous by saying she had arranged to go to the cinema with her friend, her friend's boyfriend and one of his friends. Then I started to notice she was acting even stranger. She told me that she wasn't sure if she was going out but then she did and told me she'd text me when she got back home. The next morning, I woke up to a long message saying that she'd met an incredible guy she had connected with instantly and that we hadn't had the same connection. I said to her that I respected her and appreciated her honesty.
>
> She still checks my WhatsApp status, and even updates her own instantly after I update mine. I'm a mess, what should I do, should I fight for her or let her go? She was so perfect . . . thank you for your help.
>
> Seduced and Abandoned (19)

I receive many more letters like this one: men who tell me stories I had always heard about from a woman's perspective;

men who become hopeful with someone they've just met and wonder what's going to happen, what she meant, what they should do. An interesting detail is that almost all emails sent by men begin by alluding to the difficulty of sharing these concerns: "I'm writing because I can't think of anyone that I can talk to about this." It doesn't seem like they're emasculated by these feelings, but rather that they don't know how to discuss the subject with their friends or in what situation, under which conditions.

The analysis of Geoffrey L. Greif on the difference between friendship between men and women is well-known: "Men get together and have shoulder to shoulder relationships—we do things together. In contrast, women are more adept to having face to face relationships."[13] This might be changing as I write this but, as far as I can witness, men haven't taken that step from the perplexity of the individual towards collective change. Women have had to come together in awareness groups, go out into the streets, and organize ourselves to abandon that solitary discomfort and build a situation that, though still uncomfortable, is productive in the sense that it operates at a level that supersedes the individual. I believe that men will also need to do this with hegemonic masculinity and what it has done to them, independently from women (no, we aren't going to do this for them, we aren't their teachers or carers). In the meantime, I am keeping an eye on the way in which my generation and the ones that follow question binarism, not only with ideas and words, but also with their bodies, their desire, and the nature of their feelings. An increasing number of men behave as only women did twenty years ago. And an increasing number of women behave in a way that could be characteristic of the emotional and sexual detachment Illouz speaks of—women who don't reply to messages after reading them, who leave men's houses without saying goodbye, who don't remember the men they've been with when they next bump into them. This has happened to me plenty of times. I left unanswered messages for no reason and from men who hadn't done anything wrong a long time before we had a name for this: ghosting. I once left a party with the friend of the man who had taken me there because "we were not boyfriend and girlfriend or anything like that," and I'm certain that I've behaved in this way again since then, in a way that was identical to what I experienced in the past. It's mostly clear that I did this to avoid having to tell a man that I didn't like him, that I wasn't attracted to him, that I hadn't had a good time, and that I had no intention of seeing him again. But in some cases, I behaved in this way because I understood it to be the cool approach, namely, that the trend was to behave as a man would rather than as an irritating girl. In summary, I did it because I either genuinely felt no desire for them or because I understood that was the way to become more desirable.

At surface level, it might seem as if there is a role reversal in these cases, but I believe the issue is more complex than that. Men also have emotional needs and that has always been the case. In fact, as explained by Moira Weigel when she speaks of emotional labor and by philosopher Kate Manne when she analyzes the structure of misogyny,[14] the patriarchy sets an expectation for women to offer men certain emotional effects. Not only sex, but also active listening, comprehension, recognition, respect, admiration, and nourishment for their self-esteem; things that all men and women want to a certain extent, but that appear as an obligation imparted by one on the other. A great number of these rights and duties are still a reality (we see it in the cases of men who become aggressive when a woman doesn't provide what they consider their given right for example), although the mandate of male detachment has somewhat disrupted this norm. The women who have adapted have learned to take a default detachment position too: some do so to be liked and to protect themselves and others because that's who they are—women who find opening themselves up to affection more difficult than simply having sex and leaving. Some men are attracted to that, but many others are not. Furthermore, I would go as far as to say that the real Cool Girl isn't detached. She's carefree when they want her to be and loving when they want her to be. Except for one case—one in which the man in question insisted politely until he became bored—every single time I've ghosted someone, my phone has ended up inundated with violent messages: "Are you not going to answer, you bitch?" "If you don't want to talk anymore, say it to my face, you fucking asshole," "let's see if you answer these messages, you motherfucker," "I thought you were more mature but it looks like I was wrong. In the end you're a little whore like all the rest."

I believe that this loop that repeatedly takes us from the torments of single life to an unhappy relationship is a vicious circle. Many single women I know confess to feeling desperate, literally exhausted by the challenges of singlehood: their souls are drained; their bodies, minds, self-esteem, and energy are depleted. They can no longer open up, wait, face disappointment, feel cheated and used. Of course, the grass is always greener on the other side (being in a relationship is not constantly peaceful), but sexual and emotional affection outside of monogamy could be slightly less tiresome. And perhaps if it were that way, we would have a different perspective and be less impatient to enter any relationship, whichever one, as long as it wakes us up from the nightmare of single life. We're not only eager to find a boyfriend because the romantic couple and motherhood are presented as the only tools to become socially "valued." We're eager to find a boyfriend because of the oppressive and mercantile climate that prevails in the world of single women. Freedom is always difficult and dangerous and that's partly where its beauty lies. But it would be more beautiful if it was even just a little less cruel at times.

In *Why Love Hurts*, Eva Illouz aims to leave her values and opinions out of her sociological investigation as far as possible. However, in an article published by *Haaretz*, a newspaper from Israel, she offered a fascinating defense of the importance of the couple in the contemporary world. In a world governed by autonomy and the constant search for satisfaction, the couple seems obsolete and, precisely for that reason—in her opinion—it becomes valuable. The couple is the opposite of the constant search for satisfaction. It implies renouncing the perpetual search for "something better" and learning to belong to one place, even when it isn't what we want every microsecond of our lives. It often means prioritizing the other's interests over our own, of course through our own autonomous decision, but still considering someone else's feelings and desires. I believe this to be an acute argument in favor of stable long-term bonds, but I continue to wonder whether there are ways to embody those principles (responsibility, caring for the other, setting aside one's interests) not only as a way of living outside of the romantic relationship, but also outside of what we understand as *stable bonds*. There must be a way in which single life can also be loving and caring: that someone we meet once a year can also lend their shoulder and ear on a difficult night even if there's no sex on the cards; daring to be available and open with the people in our lives even if our relationship with them has no name (yet) nor continuity; not finding it strange if a man, with whom we've shared a bed but little else, needs to tell us something or ask for something outside of that dynamic. Thinking about love and friendship in a more fluid way, as accessible examples of free union not bound by rigid rules, daily interactions, or "joint projects," but rather by sheer freedom. With these free-flowing bonds as a starting point, I want to build a communal and collective commitment with bodies and desiring people that doesn't presuppose obligations or labels, but instead demands care and affection in the most ample and truthful sense of the terms. I want to disregard the logic of consumption of people characteristic of a market where we mutually measure and rate each other, and instead attempt to face our own and the other's desire head on—when we are attracted to someone but also when we are irritated, exasperated, or confused by them.

I believe this to be a key step forward in recognizing the precarious condition of our bonds. A lack of stability does not imply a precarization of the other, uncertainty does not necessarily mean fear, and impermanence and fleetingness are not indifference but opportunities for the present to unfold.

When the newspaper I work for found out the CEO of Happn would be visiting Argentina, the editor immediately thought of me. "Go see if you can get a cover story," she said, and so I went to Plaza Hotel wearing my best shoes and with a divided heart: being asked to do a cover story is always a boost to the ego (though my friends read the articles online and never realize), but at the same time I would have preferred to do a short interview so I could save the juiciest material for myself. Or rather, for this book.

I normally prepare quite a lot before an interview, but in this case, I didn't even think it necessary. Between conversations with friends and what I had read from my agony aunt column (as well as my own experience), I believe there are only very few subjects I am more well versed in than Happn, a key competitor—today, the indisputable market leader—of Tinder and other applications used to meet people in Argentina and in the world. I even know details that cannot be written in any column: anyone can read on Wikipedia that Happn connects you with people you crossed paths with physically (on the bus; on the streets on your way to the office, or even in the office itself; at a café you frequently visit), contrary to Tinder which uses geolocation (namely, it shows people who, at the time you go online, are within a specific radius of miles). Anyone can also read that in the same way as Tinder and most apps targeting a heterosexual audience,[1] Happn allows for a conversation to begin only once both people have mutually "liked" each other and that it avoids, as other similar apps do, explicitly informing you which people you liked[2] did not like you back. However, hardly any official source will tell you that "young girls from the upper class are on Happn" because—as my techy friends explained to me—dating apps normally follow the opposite route that gentrification does: when they first launch in Argentina, they are normally in the cell phones of people who travel a lot and who have heard about them in another country, though young people can also be early adopters (pioneers). As they become more mainstream, the user base grows but becomes more "ordinary." In that critical moment a new app must appear for all the pioneers to colonize (this is effectively what is happening with Bumble, the preferred app of my younger sister that my friends aren't using yet).

I hadn't read much, then, about the story of the company and perhaps that is why I was surprised by the man who was waiting for me in one of the conference rooms of the Plaza Hotel. Didier Rappaport, the CEO in question, was nothing like the mental image I'd fabricated. He didn't look like Mark Zuckerberg, nor did he wear a Star Wars t-shirt, jogging pants, and trainers; he didn't look like a millennial nor was he one. Rappaport was then a sixty-three-year-old French man with grey hair, heavy footsteps, and a warm smile. He was tall and elegant, "handsome" as my mother would say.

Aside from the surprise and the stereotypes, the generational distance intrigued me greatly; the people I know of Rappaport's age don't use dating apps and don't want to. In general, if you explain to them how these apps work, they become bored or impatient. Some see them as promiscuous or unsafe and others as cold and impersonal.

But Rappaport has a different outlook. I believe that it was partly his peculiar point of view (free of mistrust but also free of blind optimism) that allowed him to build one of the most successful dating apps in the world. "I am French, I come from the country of love," he says with a smile on his face, then hurries to clarify that the world itself is the country of love. "We all grew up consuming the same narratives that present love as something that appears by chance, that we find when we are not looking rather than when we are. No one wants that magic to be lost. Happn is different in that respect," he explains.

He's right. Dating apps are increasingly popular among people my age (I don't think I have a single friend who hasn't used them at least once), but they're not part of anyone's fantasies: according to a survey ran by Happn on Argentinians between twenty and fifty years old, only nineteen percent think these applications are the ideal way to start a relationship. The option chosen by the majority of fifty-two percent is not being introduced by a friend nor at parties or clubs, but "destiny."

Happn's survey involved men and women, but this answer (a romantic one in traditional terms) overlaps with the way in which we, women particularly, were taught to think of love. In fact, it reminds me of an anecdote by Sam Yagan, one of the founders of an old dating website launched in 2004, which later became the app, OkCupid. Yagan tells journalist Emily Witt in *Future Sex* that one of the unsuspected benefits of the site being free of charge is that women could pretend (with others, but also with themselves) that they had not created a profile to find a boyfriend or to have sex, but instead claim they had done so because they were "curious." In that way, if they met someone, the idea that it had been pure chance could be preserved. "They say things like: 'Oh, I just met my boyfriend on OkCupid. I didn't even sign up to go on dates!' Of course, I believe you," Yagan said to Witt in an ironic tone. "Literally a third of the success emails we receive are from women—who write to the app to tell their stories and often to thank us—who include a clarification such as 'I didn't sign up to go on dates.'"[3] The paradox is that a "success email" is one that of course says "I'm in a couple." No one writes to thank the platform because they made new friends.

I believe that the idea of chance is what convinced many people who had never used dating apps in the early two-thousands to adopt Tinder and Happn a decade later. "If I had to summarize the complaints dating websites receive, I would name three things: they take too long to set up, they're too virtual, and they're generally misleading," says Rappaport. These initial services (like Match.com, a pioneer site founded in 1995 which still survives today as both a website and an app) took inspiration from "personal ads" that people used to place in newspapers and that involved creating a profile, hence taking too long to set up. Signing up meant answering a series of long questions about your preferences, professional life, life goals, and so on (which implied having all of this figured out). It's also clear why they were thought to be misleading as the details used to create a profile that would match another one were personal details which are difficult to verify. People frequently "embellished" their descriptions. And of course it's reasonable to criticize them for being "too virtual" as nothing of the physical world was included in those platforms. In fact, these kinds of platforms were frequently used to form bonds with people who lived on the other side of the world, with whom you could be corresponding for months or even years before seeing their face (if you ever did see it).

In that sense, both Tinder (founded in 2012) and Happn (created two years later) changed the rules of the game. In both cases, there was no longer a requirement to provide specific details such as favorite ice-cream flavor and professional ambitions. Downloading the app and creating a profile takes only a couple of minutes and demands minimal effort. The opportunity to lie still exists in a way because the pictures that you upload to the app can be edited or at least taken from the best angle possible, but the window for lying is small, mainly because there is a lot less information about which to lie: the only requirements are brief "bios" (optional) and age (you can lie about your age of course, but this also happens in real life). And finally, they both have a clear relationship with the physical world. In the case of Tinder, the user can choose the radius of a certain number of miles within which they want to meet people (ranging from one to one hundred miles). On Happn, this connection is even more direct as the profiles shown are of those who have crossed paths with you or, in its latest version, who you could have crossed paths with (for example, if every Tuesday you go to the same bar after therapy, Happn now shows you the profiles of the people who go to that bar every Monday). "What I wanted," explains Rappaport, "was to bring the real world back into the digital dating scene. Happn only shows you people you crossed paths with. It doesn't choose for you or tell you what to do. It doesn't tell you that because you have this or that in common, you must get married. Exactly for that reason we aren't led by algorithms and preferences. Do you like green salad? Me too. Do you think that is a reason to fall in love? Well . . . not really," he laughs.

Everything Rappaport tells me seems reasonable. But remember, I was once a millennial girl myself. I remember how, as the new millennium approached, we all shared the hope that the internet would help us find that perfect soulmate who was waiting for us on the other side of the world. The idea of meeting someone because an algorithm says that we both like to walk on the beach is not appealing to me, but how have we reached a point where we need an app to talk to people that we crossed paths with at the supermarket? And why does everything Rappaport describes as pure and agreeable nevertheless end up looking—as described in sincere conversations with my friends—a lot like carnage?

When I started high school in 2002, the internet was beginning to form part of everyday life for many people belonging to the Argentinian middle class. I didn't have a cell phone or any interest in having one (back then cell phones didn't have internet connection, they were only useful for your mother to call you to find out where you were), but I spent all the time that primitive and noisy landline connection allowed to surf the internet, send emails, and chat on MSN or ICQ.[4] "Frequently" generally meant an hour or two a day at most. Going online was not only expensive, but it also occupied the landline that my mother, a pediatrician, needed for work. Furthermore, we had—like most families I knew—only one computer that was in the living room I shared with my mother and sisters. The internet was an important part of my life, but an isolated one: a space that was separate from the rest and had clear limits. There was a moment in the day (it was actually during the night mostly) when I went online; the rest of the time I was simply offline. There was a clearly defined line between where the Web ended and real life began.

Browsing the internet was still complicated in those years. It did not have the supply of information it does today about any subject you can think of, and it wasn't as easy to find that information as it is today. Despite these limitations, the internet became an ally in many ways for me during the first years at secular school, which were extremely tough. My reactions were clumsy when I was at school: my classmates talked about music I hadn't heard of, food I hadn't eaten, places I hadn't been to. On the one hand, the internet allowed me to look for details of what they mentioned (and instantly pretend that I had always known what they were talking about), and on the other hand, it gave me time to think before talking, to embellish an anecdote, to not seem too enthusiastic nor too boring. The children of the turn of the millennium discovered something centennials would never notice, in the same way fish never think about water: the internet allowed us to control the image we showed to the rest of the world. It enabled a lie of course, but it also allowed us to interact with people without feeling exposed and gave us a kind of armor to protect us.

Many of us felt that this armor allowed us to be our true selves as the clumsy ones could become witty and the quiet ones could become funny. Without the obstacle of the body—which is always unpredictable and vulnerable, particularly when you are thirteen years old—those of us who were considered geeky had our second chance on Earth. Perhaps this is why we were the early adopters of the previous decade: in 2004, while I was browsing the internet for communities of likeminded people, those who were socially successful in the real world stayed in the real world. The internet was our territory; back then a world without Instagram, the pretty girls and good-looking boys (or "the young fancy ones" my friends look for in Happn) had no place there.

I can't stop thinking about this when I read about the experiences of teenagers today and when I see that the internet has become a place where bullying and pressure prevail. For me and for many people of my generation (those who were shy, overweight, lesbians, and gay), it offered the perfect escape from all of that. As well as providing a different way of bonding with people you knew in real life, it allowed you to interact with people you wouldn't have met otherwise but had plenty in common with—people who resembled that "true self" you had constructed as your image for those who surrounded you. Tinder, with its variable radius, would have seemed completely pointless in 2005. Back then the internet was organized around taste and preferences (the same ones that dating apps from the time used to feed search algorithms) rather than around geolocation. Distance or physical proximity were the criteria that governed real life and the point of the internet was that it defied that logic: having to connect with someone just because chance had placed them in my neighborhood or at my school seemed to me like an arbitrary limitation from my mother's time, one I wasn't willing to accept. I had no interest in meeting someone who lived five blocks away from me or the boy who waited for the bus with me in the morning. I wanted to meet someone who shared my reading interests, my philosophical concerns, my music taste, and my existential questions. And I did. I met people who lived in Mexico and Chile with whom I corresponded via email for years in *Yahoo!* fan communities[5] of Massive Attack, Radiohead, and Nietzsche (I can't contain my laughter when I remember this). I mostly lied about my age, and I never found out if others did the same. In one group, I met a boy from Berazategui, a city in Buenos Aires province, with whom I finally managed to meet and share a kiss. Years later we bumped into each other at university and we both lied to everyone about how we'd met.

I didn't stay in touch with most of these people whom I had told things I felt were my most intimate truths. I even forgot their names. When I was fifteen years old and was more well versed in secular ways, I was given permission to go out dancing. I discovered the nightlife of Buenos Aires and what at the time we called "urban tribes" (my friends the punks, the goths, or the "alternative" ones) and a space of belonging and experimentation in the physical world. My virtual relationships became flat in comparison with sex and true friendship—with girls who would take me out to the street to vomit at seven in the morning or who shared their coursework with me when I forgot to do it. I understood something that I could only put into words after reading Sherry Turkle's *Reclaiming Conversation: The Power of Talk in a Digital Age.* The friction that made me run away from real encounters and take refuge on the internet as well as those uncontrollable elements that made me nervous when I was speaking to someone face to face were the same ones that made corporeal relationships so valuable. The internet had served the purpose of helping me unlock my self-esteem, build a sense of belonging, and realize that I had something interesting to contribute to a conversation, but the body is not a secondary part of human relations and setting it aside was not a move with no implications. "From the early days," says Turkle, referring to her first research work involving adolescents and technology, "I saw that computers offer the illusion of companionship without the demands of friendship and then, as the programs got really good, the illusion of friendship without the demands of intimacy."[6]

It doesn't surprise me that as technology began permeating our lives, people began to choose programs and applications concerned with generating relationships in the physical world (such as Tinder) rather than correspondence with an online friend with whom they would never meet. However, I still believe there's a useful lesson to be learned from the comparison between the ways of bonding during the early days of the internet[7]—insufficient but representing a refuge and a safe space for many—and the present nature of social media and dating apps as toxic spaces where instead of feeling protected, we feel exposed.

In a sense, these relationships were the opposite of Tinder. I don't mean to say there was no aggression, because there was: in the forums, we would fight to the death to determine which was the best album, who had the best argument in a certain discussion or the best interpretation of this or that book. And we would frequently gang up against one person until we made them leave the community. But in those years, you connected with people and ended up learning everything about them, except for one aspect which could not come for years: what they looked like. Uploading pictures was complicated and slow, and in most of the communities it was also optional. Those who never experienced this or don't remember these forums can simply watch Nora Ephron's movie *You've Got Mail* in which the characters portrayed by Meg Ryan and Tom Hanks, mortal enemies in "real" life (she is the owner of a small bookshop in Brooklyn, and he owns an enormous chain and wants to crush her business), fall in love via emails as they exchange their impressions on books, movies, and life in general without knowing who the other is until the end. Today's most successful dating apps are the exact opposite: the only mandatory information required is your name, age, and picture. When you choose a person on Tinder or Happn in the hopes of organizing a date, that's the only information you have.

The internet was a separate and defined world; that is the key difference between 2005 and today. We used to feel safe (even though the media campaigned to warn us about the presence of pedophiles and organ sellers, messages our parents believed) because what happened there seemed not to have real-life consequences. If you argued with your community, even if you were banned (expelled), you could simply leave, and no one would know about it. You could even turn off the computer and feel that all of that disappeared. This changed with the mass adoption of social media and the advent of smartphones, which generated the necessary conditions for dating apps to appear. Pseudonyms (nicknames) that used to protect your "virtual self" from an intrusion of the physical world were replaced with the use of real names, which almost all of us use on Facebook (linked with almost all dating apps). As the internet was filled with information (increasingly easy to find thanks to Google), anonymity became almost impossible. Our parents began to use social media. Our bosses too. People lose their jobs and partners today because of things that happen on the internet and the bullying that happens there has an indistinguishable continuity with bullying at school. The internet ceased to be something we could switch off and became a mirror of our social, professional, and emotional lives in general.

Moreover, in the first decade of the year 2000 in Argentina, the internet was still a product used by the middle and upper classes, and more specifically, by young people with high educational levels. This has also changed. In 2017, only one in two Argentinians had access to a bank account, but nine out of ten owned a smartphone.[8] The dispersion of mobile technology in

our country is the highest of the region and this is repeatedly corroborated by the user data of various applications, including dating apps: Argentina is within the ten countries where Tinder is
most used. According to data shared by magazine *Infotechnology*
the application has fifteen million users in Argentina (by no
means a negligible figure in a country with forty-four million
inhabitants including children and adolescents who cannot use
it, because they are under the age of eighteen). Happn, Tinder's
nearest competitor, has two million users in the country and
Buenos Aires is the city with the fourth highest number of users
in the world. An intriguing fact that Rappaport told me is that
Buenos Aires' iconic *Obelisco* is the place where most crushes
(when two people like each other on Happn) take place in the
whole world.

But I believe there is another fundamental difference. The
internet of my adolescence was a world of text whereas the internet of today is a world of images. What most resembles the
Web of that time is Twitter, the social media network that is
constantly on the brink of insolvency where the last remaining
fans of forums and blogs go, a network that teenagers today are
not interested in in the slightest. For our successors—shy teens,
girls who dislike their bodies, and boys and girls who read a lot
and whose faces are full of spots—the internet is a hostile environment. Of course, there are still niches where they can write
fan fiction and discuss absurd obsessions like we did. But social media changed mainstream Internet forever. The Instagram
stars of today are those popular girls who in my day would have
thought that meeting people online was weird. Those hours we
spent translating song lyrics to become the most popular members of a forum would now be a waste. Today, to be popular
(on Tinder, Happn, and on Instagram, the app that was not
specifically created for dating but rather is used for everything)
those hours must be invested in the gym.

At ten in the morning on the subway, a man my age swipes profiles on Tinder. He rarely stops to look at more pictures; he does not dedicate more than one or two seconds to each profile. In general, he swipes right (the "like" side); only on one or two occasions do I see him hesitate and change direction with his finger. His expression is not one of approval or of disapproval, nor does it express hope or fun. It must be the same expression of apathy I have while I look at shoes I'll never purchase on Instagram. I'm also swiping picture after picture, waiting to see if a pair is different enough from the rest to convince me to spend my money I shouldn't be spending on something I don't need. But I don't find any. They're shoes. Some might be prettier than others, but they are all the same to a certain extent.

If the metaphor of the market of desire that Eva Illouz used sounded somewhat dark or far-fetched, dating apps turned it into an almost literal example. Compare Tinder with meeting someone at a nightclub for example: if a man comes to talk to me, asks me out to dance, or offers me a drink (thinking of a heteronormative nightclub, like most nightclubs I know, where men usually make the first move), the chances are that I will reject him or accept his offer in an instant. But the situation is likely to be more complex than that. Unless I think he is too good or bad looking to leave no margin for a change of mind, the likelihood is that I will decide if I like him or not along the way based on a multitude of factors including the things he says, his tone of voice, his body language, and how all that impacts me. What I feel toward him is tied to what I believe I provoke in him—whether he looks at me in the eye, listens to me, laughs. At the same time, he's going through a similar process. The fact that he took the initiative doesn't mean he's decided what he wants with me (thousands of times a man asked me to dance only to grow bored halfway through and say goodbye to return to his group; this does not bother me and I believe it to be acceptable if done politely). I don't want this to sound like I am idealizing nightclub flirting, which is not the panacea for any-thing—and can sometimes be violent, inconsiderate, and many more things—but I am interested in pointing out that, even if we characterize this situation as a transaction, it is precisely a *transaction between two people*. If the person in question looks at me when I speak to him with the same expression that I look at shoes on Instagram or the same expression this man on the subway has while he swipes his Tinder options, the likelihood is that the romantic transaction will instantly end in nothing. For something to ensue, there must be a mutual recognition, even if minimal, of the other's subjectivity (many aggressive men know this all too well as even if they have no intention of treating you as a person, they'll pretend they do initially). However, on dating apps, because of how the process is systematized, what you have in front of you is not a person but a profile, and a pro-file that says very little. You don't interact with it or attempt to read and understand its gestures: the profile doesn't need to be seduced nor made to feel safe or comfortable. You only need to decide, like I need to decide on the shoes, alone in front of the screen, whether to make a purchase or not.

Most of the women I know do impossible things to decode up to the last drop of information they find on a profile, as we do when we buy a t-shirt: we make sure that it doesn't contain too much polyester, we try to visualize how it will fit us in com-parison to the model who is wearing it, and if it will be as tight or as loose on us as it is on her. This is what Eva Illouz refers to when she says that in the twenty-first century—and more specifically since the beginning of online dating—the process of sexual and emotional selection is intellectualized. When facing a profile (with pictures that are usually not too sexy and seem better suited to a job application) that does not interact with me nor with my hormones, the decision I need to make is a cold one that is based on hard data and utility calculations: do I like his shirt, do I approve of the sentence he used on his bio, are his abdominal muscles sufficiently defined? On the other hand, in a nightclub or in any other "physical" situation, it used to be more common (it still happens every now and then fortunately) to decide to have sex with someone *just because*. I'm not referring to coercive situations, nor to situations in which there is no desire. I am referring to perhaps the most genuine desire, that of having sex with a man who does not seem handsome, cool, or correspond in the least with what you think attracts you intellectually. Choosing to have sex with a man just because you felt like it, because the body and the moment asked for it, because it seemed like a good idea. For better or for worse (and this is not a value judgement), Tinder is the opposite of this— one could begin to like profiles in a random manner and the process would still have nothing to do with the uncontrollable chance of unconscious desire. The process cannot be physical on Tinder because there are no bodies there, hence it can be nothing other than intellectual, even if all it offers is pictures. That is what the pictures are. The internet is full of pictures but not full of bodies. Those pictures are not bodies. This is why I often think of Tinder as a market, but never as a "meat market." If only there was more meat involved.

Just as Eva Illouz relates contemporary love to consumerism in *Labor of Love*, Moira Weigel links it to work. This metaphor also becomes an explicit one with dating apps and flirting in the age of social media. For Weigel (who admitted the implicit alignment of her views with Marxist feminism in interviews),[9] love has always been a part of female tasks, as Silvia Federici confirms,[10] but it mutated in the same way productive labor did. Dating increasingly feels like a job interview. Viewing a profile on Tinder might feel like considering whether to purchase a t-shirt, but it also feels like the search for "the best candidate for the role." It's no longer about "chemistry" (there can't be any with just pictures) but rather about meeting certain requirements.

I recognize myself in the characterization of "finding who to have sex with and making it happen" as a job. In 2013, before Tinder arrived in Argentina, I had created my own Tinder. I used to sit in front of Facebook once a week and look among friends of friends for boys I thought were good looking and relatively cool and send them a friend request. At least one out of two ended up saying hello and, out of those, two out of three asked me out. I explained my method to every girl who complained about not going on enough dates. They were all in awe of my system, half fascinated and half disgusted. I had not read Weigel's book (which had not been written yet), but I was already saying: "It's like a job." Add enough boys, start liking their posts, comment every now and then, monitor their activity so as not to forget to pay them some attention but not too much for it to seem excessive. It would have been easier to simply approach the one I liked without so much performance, but that is where the irony lies: that necessity Emily Witt speaks of, the need for everything to seem like a beautiful coincidence that requires no effort, desire, or willingness. Often the most laborious task within the female labor of love is not exposing the fact that you are actually working.

That concealment of effort exerted on finding sex or love is not only done for others, but also for oneself. My Facebook routine, expressed in figures and probabilities, neutralized the exposure flirting facilitates that I often found unbearable. The fear of rejection is so consuming that Tinder and Happn simply eliminated it, and you can no longer find out whether someone swipes your profile to the "do not like" side. The intellectualization of these processes—that often happens in the subconscious as we can think of flirting as an experience of consumerism or labor, but we rarely explicitly call it that—*protects* us from the sense of vulnerability generated by exhibiting and pursuing our own desire. But, just like any other attempt to protect the precarious condition of living, it is futile. We feel secure in the neatly organized interface that hides the other's desire and rejection, but reality always breaks through the smooth surface of any fantasy in the end. That boy who liked your profile never answered your message, the one who said hello disappeared when you didn't agree to go straight to his house and proposed going for a coffee first instead, the one who got angry because you took too long to answer his messages (why did you pretend to be interested?), the boy who accused you of lying with your profile picture after seeing a few other pictures on Facebook, and the fifth boy you simply didn't like.

The application and its system of matches or crushes, or whatever each app calls these encounters, promised a lack of tension, rejection, and misunderstandings, but this did not happen. Instead it took away a vital aspect: the chance to show others how you move, how you speak, who you are, what it feels like to spend time with you. If you had this opportunity, perhaps things would be different. Maybe that boy who "missed out on you" (because deep down you know that you liked his profile and he did not choose you as he never showed as a match, although apps do all within their reach to make you forget about this) would have given you a chance. But the apps don't offer that possibility, or even allow you to charm him with a seductive conversation as was once the case in chatrooms, or with your great arguments about the last B side of Radiohead, as once was the case in the forums and mail groups I use to join. All you can do is suck in your stomach for the picture, pray that you're young enough for someone to be interested in talking to you, and choose a Tweet-sized sentence that no one will read. Instead of being protected, these limitations make you feel even more naked.

Aside from the metaphors of consumerism and labor, there is another idea I hadn't thought of as it doesn't form part of daily practices but is a habit often found in the education and subjectivity of men my age: dating apps resemble videogames.

I first came across this comparison in *Men, Masculinity and Contemporary Dating*, a recent book by Chris Haywood, specialist in masculinity. Haywood did a series of comprehensive interviews with fifteen boys aged between eighteen and twenty-four in order to analyze their practices and perceptions on Tinder. He contrasted them with the best available bibliography on the subject to elaborate various hypotheses on the way in which young men are using the application. As Max, nineteen, puts it: "I think a lot of game apps get boring quite quickly as well. So, Tinder is constantly refreshing, and you've always got new people on there, new faces. So, it feels more like a game to pass the time than anything else, I think. I don't expect to get anything out of it."[11]

I recognized the boy in the subway and many of my male friends in that reasoning. What interested me the most from this book was noticing that there are not only plenty of ways to use these applications, but also that the ways of using them are gendered. As a woman who shares her experiences on Tinder with other women, I always assumed that the dating app practices of my male friends would be an extension of our own. The clearest example is the habit that many men have of liking almost all the girls they see, or at least more than those they would be willing to ask out. "Why did he like my profile and then stop answering?" is a repeated question I receive at the agony aunt column, to which I answer with a particularly female intuition: that men who say yes to many options do so to increase their chances of a match. In some cases, and in some ways, that is true, but it's not the full story. Sometimes they say yes to all profiles just because, like playing Mortal Kombat on the arcade machines, they press all the buttons without looking. It's not an exaggeration to say that we women take Tinder seriously—as we're bombarded with messages that are pro-monogamy, anti-singlehood, and anti-casual sex (often combined into one, for example in phrases such as "Why buy a cow when you can get the milk for free?"). Liking a boy is something we consider carefully. Like purchasing a fridge, a computer, or another expensive item, you must choose well as there is another cost involved: if you like a boy and then you are not willing to go out with him, you will likely have to endure a few insistent and aggressive messages. Instead, Tinder can be more like a videogame for a man, something to look at when you're bored "without expecting to get anything from it."

This "playful" attitude, different to the way women are considered to behave on Tinder, is not as innocent as it seems. Haywood writes that whilst men have often viewed dating through a lens of competition, the framing of such competition through the navigation of a mobile app points to notions of play that are associated with gaming, consoles, and video games. This 'game' format, Haywood continues, protects men from a sense of vulnerability. The application allows them to believe that what happens in there does not count in real life to a certain extent.

A crucial aspect of masculinity—Haywood explains, quoting sociologist Janet Holland's work—is that it stems from the way in which men exert their power over women and dictate the conditions on which a relationship can develop. This characterization is reminiscent of how Illouz explains masculine indifference as a form of control. Men feel vulnerable during a sexual encounter for many reasons, such as the pressure of measuring up to the cultural ideal of hegemonic masculinity (strength, power), the possibility of opening up to emotional dependance on another person, and also because the ideal of female passivity they learned is replaced by a real, desiring body that threatens their traditional role. Men have historically adopted various strategies to overcome this insecurity: seeking affirmation from their peers (by sending a picture of a girl they have just been with to the WhatsApp group with the caption "look at what I'm eating"), or labelling women in a negative way (these are those who ask you for a dance, then when you reject them they call you fat, ugly, or a whore). For Haywood, the way in which Tinder is used integrates these masculine strategies that tend to neutralize that vulnerability that is so incompatible with hegemonic masculinity: "the gamification of dating becomes a means of creating emotional distance and investment in relationships. The result is that young men, through tropes of consumption and gamification, reinforce structures of objectification and structures of patriarchy."[12]

The metaphors of consumerism, labor, and videogames all point in the direction of dehumanizing the other. To protect ourselves from the potential pain and anxiety caused by being exposed as desiring and vulnerable beings, some of us imagine that we are accumulating candidates as if we were Human Resources managers, some compare them to a fridge, and others to a collection of avatars. In all those cases, the *fear of humanity* leads us to attempt to forget the other's humanity, which has its consequences mainly because dating apps do not operate in a void: they are superimposed with a relationship dynamic with a (patriarchal, heteronormative, and mononormative) history that unavoidably permeates through the ways in which we use them. Women and men repeat the relationship patterns and behaviors we've learned from Tinder, Happn, Bumble, or whichever dating app we use. And perhaps virtuality leaves less room than real life for opportunities to participate in genuine encounters and learn how to subvert these dynamics.

In *Down Girl: The Logic of Misogyny*,[13] philosopher Kate Manne analyzes how throughout history, women have been taught to treat men with deference, kindness, and even affection by default. When, talking about consent, we say that *no is no*, we don't just mean men accepting a negative response. We must also speak of the need to create the space for women to feel that there is room for a negative response, that we have a right to say *no* without being afraid of the consequences. Journalist

Dave Schilling researched the difference between the reasons why women and men *ghost* for men's magazine *MEL Magazine*. Drawing upon a series of surveys and interviews, he discovered that most heterosexual women do it not because they disregard the other person's feelings, but because they fear how the man will react to a clear and honest negative response.[14] Technology offers the opportunity to avoid a situation that might end up in insults, persistence, or violence. At the same time, however, this shortcut increases our precarious condition (and it often doesn't benefit us in any way). It invites us to accept that saying *no* is a problematic situation, one that we should be afraid of. Ghosting means accepting that we have no right to say "yes" or "no": the words must be whispered, smuggled in. It means accepting that we must apologize for our desire, for wanting to have sex, and also for not wanting to. It is accepting that we cannot talk about sex freely because the conversation around heterosexual desire must remain in the dark, be confusing, and bashful.

Men, instead—as Illouz and Haywood found—socialize within the belief that emotional detachment and indifference towards women's feelings warrant power and allow them to keep control of the relationship. In the interviews Haywood conducts, the boys he speaks to seem to not even consider the feelings of the girls they match with on Tinder. For example, they believe trolling (making scatological jokes before even saying hello) to be not only funny, but also relatively harmless.

Haywood analyzed another common practice among young men, the collective use of Tinder. "During the interviews," he writes, "it became evident that one of the ways of using Tinder was a shared activity between groups of friends." The mobility of the smartphone, the possibility of looking at someone who doesn't know she's being looked at and the fact that her image can be captured and shared with friends, means that these apps are not only used to meet girls, but also as a homosocial tool among men. Homosociality, which is simply an interaction between members of the same gender, is not by definition patriarchal or negative; it can create space for support, affection, intimacy, and solidarity. But in a group of men who discuss pictures of women and comment on whether they are fat or seem like an easy conquest, there might be affection and comradery, but there is also humiliation and the formation of a habit. And although these girls never find out (sometimes they do, if the picture is shared on social media and becomes viral on the internet), this practice influences the subjectivity of the men who take part in it. "Although this does not necessarily lead to misogynist and objectifying behavior," Haywood explains, "the practice creates a sense of non-empathy that allows men to treat and use women as objects."[15]

I believe that this explanation perfectly captures the correlation between technology and the bonding habits this technology promotes. Tinder *is not guilty* of preventing men from seeing women as people; in fact, it might even be capable of fostering a respectful way of using a dating app. But these tools enable interactions that can lead to new ways of increasing the precarity of other people by virtue of a particular characteristic they share: ignoring that bodies are part of every emotional interaction. In *Reclaiming Conversation*, Sherry Turkle explains that face-to-face interaction is irreplaceable when it comes to learning about empathy: there is no number of text messages that can replace what we learn to feel from the other's body in a face-to-face, body-to-body conversation. Her arguments are based on empirical psychology, but they remind me of the ethics of philosopher Emmanuel Levinas, who views the face as the way in which we present ourselves. Levinas believes the face belongs to a metaphysical and ethical category: it highlights the nakedness of the other, their vulnerability, and our responsibility towards them. The face defies all description: Levinas does not refer to the face as we generally understand it, as a combination of features or a sum that can be described. In fact, he believes that considering a person's concrete features implies an objectification: "The best way of encountering the Other," he writes in *Ethics and Infinity*, "is not even to notice the color of his or her eyes."[16]

I search in my memory, I can barely remember the eye color of anyone I have desired with my whole body. What comes to mind when I think of those encounters are feelings, not *information*. I remember the details of a boy I was looking at on Instagram yesterday but will most likely never see in real life. I feel the same way about other experiences that are untransferably human and physical such as my favorite teachers from school and university: I remember the kindness with which they explained topics, I recall a feeling of being very present in the moment and a need to absorb everything that was happening. I also remember a lot of what I learned though the learning is unconnected to the experience. When I explain these concepts in a lecture or use them in an article, my body always returns to the first feeling they manifested in me—the attentive smile of the teacher, our eyes meeting as I was learning.

A lot of people I know refuse to use dating apps. They believe them to be cold, boring, and objectifying, stripping away the fun and erasing the element of eroticism, essentially rendering them useless. Though hardly anyone claims they don't use them because they don't need them. "When you ask people why they are single," Rappaport asked me, "what do they normally answer?" We both answered his question simultaneously: "meeting people is hard." This is by far what my friends repeat most frequently, although it comes as no surprise if we consider the demographic, social, and political transformation of recent decades.

In *Modern Romance*, actor Aziz Ansari[17] and anthropologist Eric Klinenberg decided to research romance in the twenty-first century by asking older residents living in a care home in New York how they had met their husbands and wives. The answers surprised them. In one of the most cosmopolitan cities in the world, almost all the residents had married people who lived within walking distance of their homes. Many even married neighbors living in their same building or same block. After comparing the data, they corroborated that this was not a coincidence. They had also married at a much younger age than people today do (at least ten years younger on average, in their early twenties instead of early thirties) and, when they were asked why they had married their respective partners, they rarely answered with the epic tales Ansari's friends narrated when talking about their marriages. They did not say "she is perfect for me, I love everything she loves, and she loves everything I love" but instead they shared statements such as "he was a good man," "I liked his family," "he was kind and hard-working," "she was industrious, and my mother liked her." One woman even said that, although her husband and her understood each other very well, they were very different, and she frequently asked herself what her life would have been like if she had married someone who shared her interests.[18]

Meeting people is difficult for a myriad of reasons. Many of us remain single for many years after finishing high school and even university—those of us who were fortunate enough to be able to attend university. We have no community ties with the people from our neighborhoods (we would not need Happn to talk to them if we did); we no longer form part of religious institutions or communities of Italian, Spanish, Armenian, or Irish descendants as our parents and grandparents did (my mother and father met at the synagogue for example). We also live in an extremely socially and socioculturally stratified society which—despite marrying people from our neighborhoods—means that the options for exploring are quickly exhausted: the boys I met in bars, clubs, or online often came from somewhat different social backgrounds than mine. However, the friends of friends I often ended up dating, were very much like me. They all know each other or could know each other, they've all attended similar educational institutions, they work in similar companies, and they have at least ten friends in common on Facebook. My friends no longer ask me to introduce them to boys as they know all my friends. They've seen them hundreds of times and they have already kissed the ones they liked. Perhaps if we were in the fifties, they would have settled for them. But because today men and women want to be swept off their feet and die for love we need a lot more options to try and test. Dating apps come to occupy the role bars and clubs used to (and still do though to a lesser extent)[19]: they offer a "new set" of people among which to look for our other half, be it forever or for that night.

It is impossible to know if dating apps as we know them are here to stay, but meeting people online certainly is—in whichever way. I don't wish to appear to be against them, because I'm not. Nor do I believe that it makes much sense to be either in favor or against them. It's like being in favor of rain or against sadness: they exist. The real question is how we personally and collectively navigate them.

I think we can extract some interesting points from these field experiments that we're the protagonists of. A promising point is the question of diversity. As Modernism progressed, the market of desire began broadening to include more people, therefore generating a new set of standards that in many cases overlaps with class and ethnic criteria, but not exclusively so. Beauty for example, is an autonomous criterion when selecting a sexual partner (someone can choose a sexual partner depending on their appearance without worrying too much about their financial situation). Dating apps integrate this process in a clear way as many of the boys interviewed by Haywood do when discussing Tinder and what they call random girls they meet on the app (many of my male and female friends use the same word to convey a sense of "any," often used in a derogatory way). Random girls or boys come from outside of your social circle and it is improbable that you will cross paths with them on Facebook or Instagram. In general, the term refers to people who do not share your code of conduct nor belong to your social class, your ethnic group, or your cultural field. This kind of distance, as evidenced in Haywood's interviews, seems to leave room for a sense of impunity when hurting someone, but also a certain effortlessness when it comes to the date: the certainty that whatever happens, no one within your group will find out, takes the weight off your shoulders. Aside from this advantage, I believe that encounters with random people could be positive not because they help to increase our options, but because they are an opportunity to build bonds with diverse people whom we would have not met in other ways, which could result in a flow of communication with other realities and a strengthening of our empathic qualities. Many of these applications take their data from our social media so that the algorithms can rank your appearance in an attempt to show your profile to people who are "as attractive" as you are (the goal for these applications is that we all go on plenty of dates). In doing this, they are likely to reproduce privileges, inequality, and bubbles. However, despite these algorithms, almost all users still encounter people who are outside of their circles and who don't frequent the spheres they belong to. These small, random opportunities that the internet creates are the place where we could find something as valuable as what happened to me when I was young and—in the affluent neighborhood of Barrio Norte in Buenos Aires—befriended the son of low-income workers from the periphery of the city because we had both joined the same anime forum.

Haywood studies another interesting point that relates to masculinity: all men and women exhibit their bodies equally on these applications, so men have to get used to being on display. Women have known for a long time what it feels like to be validated and compared by virtue of their physical beauty, but this is new for men. This observation coincides with the urgency—which also appeared in the last decade—present in the market of male beauty products and fitness, and with the reinforcement of the value of beauty (with its own parameter, but beauty still) for men in general. In principle, there seem to be no positive effects caused by men's newly established relationship with the inequality generated by the privilege of subjective beauty, but the future intrigues me. Firstly because it implies a deviation from traditional masculinity, where beauty was identified with femininity; secondly because—and one could laugh at my optimism, but I write this seriously—I wonder if men, after understanding the emotional implications of the segregation of the pretty and the ugly, will realize how horrific this system of privileges is and will join those of us who question it, or at least will find it easier to empathize with women who know what it feels like to have their bodies analyzed, observed, and constantly criticized.

I keep returning to empathy, which has no synonyms nor substitutes. We will continue to build bonds on the internet and in unconceivable ways, but we need to think of how to do this without mutually increasing our precarity and that of our relationships. Without allowing the fact that the other person is not physically present to make us forget that they exist, that they feel, and that they suffer. This is not as simple as it may sound and I believe that the answer, at least for me, lies in the body.

I'm not nostalgic: I tend to be in favor of novelty, but it's worth creating some distance between blind optimism and critical thinking on how this serves our purpose and what we should be careful of. In 2018, I interviewed Thomas Friedman, three-time Pulitzer Prize winner and war correspondent, who dedicates his time to thinking about the era of technological advancement. From this conversation, I took with me a sentence and a small anecdote that are also in one of his books. "As everything is getting faster," he said to me, "that which is old and slow matters more." Friendship, love, being a good teacher and a good parent to your children, being a good member of your community. To illustrate this, he told me the story of a conversation he had with Wael Ghonim, better known as the Google Guy—one of the key figures of the Egyptian revolution against Hosni Mubarak in 2011. "We could not have launched the revolution without Facebook," said Ghonim, "but we could not succeed with Facebook." The same medium that allowed so many people to meet each other despite the physical distance also stimulated fights and disagreements among them. We often forget that it's not easy to create an online community. The same technology that helps us communicate also alienates us if we lose sight of the fact that, to build real bonds (relating to romance, friendship, community, and politics), we need to return to the physical world.

I also think of the success of grocery delivery applications (such as Rappi and Glovo in Argentina), companies that exploit desperate laborers and take advantage of millennials who do not want to even see the face of a cashier in a shop. We need to rebel against what we call comfort but is in fact a fear of human interaction, both in individual and collective terms. The only way to learn how to talk to girls is by talking to girls, the only way to learn how to speak on the phone is by speaking on the phone, the only way to learn how to have sex is by having sex. I considered different ways of generating empathy hundreds of times, but for now the most logical approach seems to be looking for clues in old traditions and seeing how that emotional and sexual education—learning through the body, the face, and closeness—nourishes our cybernetic ways. Perhaps, if we look into enough pairs of eyes, it will be easier to remember that the eyes of that girl or boy from the app, even if we can only see them in two dimensions in the picture, also cry and become irritated, and their pupils also dilate when there isn't enough light.

I would say it all began with Twitter, but it had already begun with Instagram. Looking at influencers—and not only "famous" TV actresses, but ordinary girls with a lot of followers—I noticed their skin seemed much more radiant and flawless than mine. I always thought I had good skin: during my teenage years, I barely had any acne, never liked sunbathing, and my complexion has always been even. Yes, I've always had dark circles under my eyes, which seemed to darken with age, but overall, I feel lucky with my skin. With just minimal care, it meets the standard of what's considered desirable.

In recent years, the standards have shifted. It's partly due to Photoshop, but also because those who truly commit to skincare radiate a unique glow. One day, on Twitter, I came across a conversation between two users only slightly older than me. They discussed treatments they underwent such as monthly radiofrequency facials, mesotherapy every three weeks (less than that is equivalent to not doing it at all), injections of hyaluronic acid, "a tiny bit" of Botox "only every now and then, when I feel tempted to." This provided me with a kind of relief—I wasn't crazy, there *was* a secret. Or many secrets consisting of lasers and needles, homemade or at a clinic, with or without anesthesia.

The girls on Twitter recommended starting these treatments as early as possible if you wanted to be "in good shape" by the time you reach your forties. The internet suggested starting in your twenties, so I decided to get going. I wrote a direct message to an influencer I liked, someone I'm acquainted with and who was knowledgeable in the subject. She shared the number of her dermatologist and, rather than put it off forever, I booked an appointment for the following week.

I realize now that I didn't book the appointment thinking I would *really* go through with all these treatments. My secret expectations were that the doctor would say "you're very young and your skin is perfect. Don't do anything to it, take this cream and come back in five years." But that never happens or at least it wasn't what happened to me. The dermatologist, a young blonde woman, friendly and impeccably dressed, invited me to sit down and asked me why I had come to her clinic. I remembered a similar situation at the gym when I was a teenager, the trainer and the question had made me feel the same sense of bewilderment. The dermatologist and the trainer both wanted me to tell them what bothered me about myself: my thighs, rosacea, my strength, wrinkles, my weight, spots. I decided to give her the same answer I had given before: "I don't know. I came because I thought it was time to come." When she insisted, I mentioned my age, expression lines and *perhaps the bags under my eyes*.

"I can give you a depigmentation cream for that for now . . . and in one or two years we can do some Botox," she said naturally and—I'm sure—with no ill meaning. The words "some Botox" were imprinted in my mind. The indefinite determiner "some" seemed to be there to take the weight off the sentence, almost as if she had said "a little Botox." "I'll also prescribe a cream for the blackheads on your nose," she continued, as I tried to get a closer look at them. "And we can begin with mesotherapy and diamond tip microdermabrasion every three weeks, how does that sound?" I nodded without blinking. I was shocked and worried. Perhaps most girls had already thought about all their faults by the time they went to the clinic, but I honestly hadn't. I had gone there to *prevent*; I did not know I already needed a cure.

After the first consultation came the first session: tiny needles that hurt only slightly and a facemask. I had hoped it would be as relaxing as a spa or something of the sort, but it wasn't. The doctor made conversation, everything happened quickly and under bright lights. The session lasted two hours from the moment I arrived, began the treatment, and then left. Scheduling these sessions wasn't easy. I paid what I considered to be an absurd amount of money and went back home feeling empty. The prospect of having to go back every month was ridiculous; I felt tired, and the numbers didn't add up. Besides, it seemed excessive for my lifestyle. I do yoga and go to the gym a couple of times a week, but looking after my face as if I was a model when I don't even take exercise seriously seemed as pointless as washing the dishes with the most expensive soap and cold water. I began to consider that chasing beauty wasn't my thing, but this wasn't an easy realization to accept. I didn't find it easy to acknowledge that the cost of prettiness would increase every year; that I would be left behind while those who "did their homework," those who made the effort to do things right, those who sacrificed their time, money, and pleasure, would continue to be desired and admired with a shower of "likes." I couldn't accept it but I couldn't carry on doing all of that if I wanted to be true to myself.

The hypocrisy surrounding beauty standards is reaching levels that are difficult to endure. In the nineties, when I was a kid, the message was clear: being pretty is important, being thin is important, being young or looking young is important. Kate Moss unashamedly said that "nothing tastes as good as skinny feels," magazine covers exhibited Nicole Neumann's baby face alongside the masthead "Sexy at the age of twelve" denoting a socially accepted undertone of pedophilia that today we find shocking. It's true that hypocrisy that screams "I don't look after myself, I eat hamburgers every day, it's just my metabolism!"

is still present today, predominantly among those who hide the efforts required to adhere to the beauty canon. But in general, there were no doubts or contradictions in relation to the importance of beauty, which was understood in the frame of a very specific ideal.

This has changed in recent years. We now live with the intriguing discourse of self-acceptance. Women's magazines, celebrities, and actors narrate on their social media accounts a kind of spiritual journey that led them to love themselves and their bodies. Though in most cases, these women who preach self-love are extremely thin, toned, have straight hair, and regularly undergo massages, radiofrequency, and Botox treatments. Moreover, these women probably invest a lot more time and money in their beauty than their mothers did. The only difference is that instead of talking about calories they talk of self-love. Is this progress? I've been asking myself this question for years and I increasingly feel that I want to answer *no*.

Journalist Amanda Hess caused controversy in 2018 when she introduced the concept of Beauty-Standard Denialism in an article in *The New York Times*.[1] In a review of the somewhat forgettable movie starring Amy Schumer about a girl who one day hits her head and begins to "believe" that she is thin, Hess tackles the myth that goes hand in hand with the self-love message: affirming that what matters is your attitude, self-confidence, *how you feel*, and *what you project*. That the world doesn't marginalize you, that no one is judging you, excluding you, nor criticizing your body—it is all in your head. "That attitude," writes Hess, "puts the onus on individual women to improve their self-esteem instead of criticizing societal beauty standards writ large. The reality is that expectations for female appearances have never been higher. It's just become taboo to admit that."

A lot of people might read a story like the one I used to open this chapter and think: "Grow up. It doesn't matter if you don't want to diet and work out, no one will make you, it's your problem if you worry too much about it."

This is effectively one of the key arguments of denial: If you suffer because you feel you don't belong but think you should, it's your fault, and you have to deal with it yourself. You are the problem, not the world. If you don't fit in and you believe that implicates professional, social, emotional, and even political marginalization, then why not do the work? Start running, give up carbohydrates, go to the dermatologist, *look after yourself*, *love yourself*. Whether you're lazy or a hypocrite, the blame always lies with you.

And the worst part is that this is not an external message we receive from other people, this is a discourse that we have internalized to the extent that we struggle to distinguish it from what we want, from who we are. Sometimes I feel that, while feminism is all well and good, it would be much easier to just work on myself and take care of what truly matters. This is why I look for treatments, buy the best body creams I can afford, start diets one after the other, and spend hours Googling information about the endless list of things to do to be as beautiful as I can possibly manage.

At a feminist group meeting on the subject, someone I didn't know expressed this eloquently: "we come here, we read about beauty standards, we speak of fat activism and how we should stop shaving, we talk about rebelling, resisting, and all that, but then we think 'someone else can start,' right? No one wants to be the pioneer, the martyr. Let someone else start this, I want to carry on being thin and feminine and beautiful, and only talk about this subject. I want to carry on being desired by hegemonic males and collecting likes. Others can start, I'll join them later."

*The Beauty Myth,* by American writer Naomi Wolf, is the first book to apply feminist critique to hegemonic beauty standards. It was published in 1990 and became an instant best-seller. Although the text has some issues regarding its empirical basis that several specialists have pointed out,[2] the essence of its analysis continues to be enlightening and relevant almost thirty years later.

The concept of beauty, and in particular of beauty as a female attribute, is undoubtedly dated. However, what Wolf calls the *beauty myth* has strengthened as mass media and consumer societies emerged and expanded. "Before the development of technologies of mass production—daguerreotypes, photographs, etc.—an ordinary woman was exposed to few such images outside of the Church," writes Wolf. The legend of Helen of Troy's beauty is a few thousand years old but women of the eighth century B.C. only heard of her beauty through linguistic formulations. They hadn't *seen* it. The daily practice of comparing our bodies to those of other women, whether real or imaginary, is neither ancestral nor timeless; it's linked to a specific historical and technological moment.

Moreover, being pretty didn't play a central a role as it does today when it comes to determining the allure of a woman. "Since the family was a productive unit and women's work complemented men's," says Wolf, referencing the time that preceded the development of capitalism, "the value of women who were not aristocrats or prostitutes lay in their work skills, economic shrewdness, physical strength, and fertility. Physical attraction, obviously, played its part; but 'beauty' as we understand it was not, for ordinary women, a serious issue in the marriage marketplace."[3] This analysis goes hand in hand with the automatization of the spheres of love and sex tied to the financial and social structures Eva Illouz talks about. Beauty is today one of the key standards considered when selecting a woman as a sexual or emotional partner, and it gains importance in the marriage marketplace when love becomes independent of the criteria linked to work and financial convenience.

The tendencies Wolf speaks of have become more deeply ingrained since 1990. We're surrounded by even more images than in the times of graphic magazines and television. We take our phones to bed, to the bathroom, on public transport, even to meetings where we're supposed to be talking to other people. And not only that, from the origins of the internet and particularly of social media, images stopped being simply something that we consumed and became a central part of the way in which we relate to others. I spent a long time thinking of where to place an essay on beauty within a book about relationships: I knew it was essential, but I finally understood why only halfway through my research. On Tinder, Instagram, Happn, Bumble, Tumblr, TikTok, and the app that will be in fashion by the time this book goes to print, our photographs are the face we present of ourselves and, increasingly so, our only face. When you meet people "in real life" (at university, at work, a friend of a friend that you regularly see at parties) beauty could play a secondary role. A man who didn't find you attractive the first time he saw you could be attracted to your sense of humor, your conversation, or a certain vibe—something warm that your presence exudes. None of this can appear in a photograph, yet there's an increasing number of relationships that begin with a photograph and stay in that phase for weeks or months until a physical meeting can be organized. I get sent many questions related to this at the agony aunt column: "We've been chatting for weeks, but he hasn't suggested meeting," "we always agree to meet but then something happens, and we don't," "he asks me to send him pictures but then, when I suggest going out, he doesn't reply." Our photographs now play a pivotal role in capturing and consistently holding others' attention throughout all our interactions, navigating through all the chats and other hurdles we must overcome for a *real* encounter to materialize. I don't believe that purely visual attraction, bereft even of the presence of a body, was ever as important in the sexual and emotional market as it is today.

And there's more. Telecommunication isn't the only technology that has advanced in recent decades, contributing to the
importance of maintaining a specific physical appearance. The
information on nutrition (at times validated by science and at
times not so much) that floods social media—the increasingly
varied offer of exercises that promise the best results and are
available in every corner of the internet; the creams that promise to stop wrinkles, stretch marks, cellulitis, and any other
evidence of the life of our skin; the so-called non-invasive treatments, and the industry of plastic surgery, have all become more
sophisticated and ordinary. Products and procedures that used
to be attainable for women in show business exclusively (and I
am not necessarily thinking of the most eccentric treatments: a
Hollywood wax is a good enough example) are now part of the
everyday life of many women who work as receptionists, doctors, lawyers, waiters, teachers, or any other profession.

Does this mean that today's women more closely resemble
the public icons of beauty than in the past? I don't think so.
Although celebrity culture has skyrocketed in recent years (we
no longer compare ourselves with actors—any beautiful girl
who takes photographs in her house is a potential ideal) and
the possibility of having the "perfect" body is becoming less exclusive, most women continue to fail to embody the hegemonic
beauty standards: we are a little too fat, a little too flat-chested,
a little too short, a little too wrinkled, a little too grey-haired,
a little too flabby. But we do resemble our referents in one respect: we try as hard as we can to achieve this, with our whole
souls, bodies, and wallets. What was once dismissed as trivial
("a particularly feminine frivolity") or even as a sin of vanity,[4]
is today seen as a duty. Dieting, going to the gym, and going
to the dermatologist once a month equates to good behavior.
Most of us don't resemble Gwyneth Paltrow or Argentine actor
China Suárez, but what matters is that we do what they do, as
much as our possibilities allow. It was also Wolf who said that

it is the beauty myth, rather than appearances, that constantly prescribes behaviors.

In her book, Wolf speaks of beauty as a new religion, dictating how we should care for and treat our bodies. In the book *Perfect Me: Beauty as an Ethical Ideal*[5] published in 2018, philosopher Heather Widdows summarizes and unpacks this argument, considering what has happened in the beauty sector in the last decade. Instead of a religion, Widdows speaks of ethics: if being "good" once meant resisting the temptation of premarital sex or praying every morning and every night, today, "putting in the hard work" means waking up early to go to the gym and saying "no" to that tempting slice of chocolate cake. Speaking of ethics might seem like an exaggeration, but I think this is quite an accurate characterization: the vocabulary we use today to refer to keeping our bodies in shape is increasingly moralistic. My friends and I do as many "bad" things as any other generation; we cancel plans with a friend, shout at someone, lie, or say something hurtful to our partners. However, most frequently when we talk about guilt, we focus on what we've eaten or the fact that we haven't gone for a run because it was cold outside.

How can one uphold these beauty ethics without it feeling like it is a matter of utmost stupidity for relatively functioning adults? One correlation facilitates this: the increasingly strong relationship between beauty and health in the public discourse. The narrative of self-acceptance (or the denial of beauty standards, if we prefer to call it that) prevents us from speaking openly of how much we would love to weigh twenty pounds less than we do or how much we would love to have an ass like Ariana Grande's. But there's nothing wrong with me saying that I want to "feel better," "eat more healthily," or even "feel good about myself." These statements are often left unchallenged: nobody asks why feeling better always means being thinner (if you're not overweight, why would being thinner be better, or why is having a firmer butt "healthier?"). Or why "eating healthily" is code for "eating less," or why I need to look a certain way to feel good about myself.

On the one hand, the discourse surrounding health is indisputable as we would all like to be healthy. But on the other hand, there is an increase in the popularity of the idea that criticizing a certain practice is a personal attack on those women and not particularly sisterly behavior, or that questioning their decisions is disrespecting their freedom. "We can all do whatever we want," many women answer when a feminist attempts to discuss the subject. In the prologue of the second edition of *The Beauty Myth* Naomi Wolf writes that she found a lot of this kind of resistance coming from television presenters who felt offended by the affirmation that women must be beautiful to be given a space on screen, as if they didn't have any agency or power to make decisions. And who, as a feminist, would want to question another woman's personal choices?

Given that the personal is rarely stripped away from political undertones, we will continue to face these thorny discussions, and I don't believe that we should avoid them or disparage them by saying that "we can all do whatever we want." We all do what we *want*, but also what we *can*, and what we can do is conditioned by political, economic, and cultural factors. that affect us collectively in various ways, and that we can only confront together by creating a dialogue around them. It's not about pointing fingers, but about thinking collectively of the circumstances that lead us to make personal decisions today.

The narratives of self-acceptance, health, and individual freedom all have one thing in common: they stop the conversation and hide our collective anxieties and pain. They also conceal the multimillionaire businesses that earn their fortunes by feeding these anxieties while promising to solve them. These narratives make us feel as though we're imagining things, as though we're crazy, paranoid, or that we let easily solvable trivialities make us suffer. But most of all, they make us feel alone. These narratives emphasize individuality while obscuring the societal forces that structure our most private opinions on our own bodies—*I* need to learn to accept myself as I am, *I* need to be better because of my health "rather than because of aesthetics," *I* want to be hungry and deny myself of what I like because *I* can choose freely. And, if you feel that something about this doesn't sound quite right or that it isn't good for you, *you* are the problem. These ways of thinking are what lead you up that blind alley.

Heather Widdows attempts, as Naomi Wolf did before, to change the focus of this conversation. By speaking of ethics, the onus lies on the individual decision of each woman rather than on the system that limits and gives meaning to their choices. Widdows uses the word "ethics" in a philosophical sense that is both precise and generic to refer to a moral perspective and a duty that determines what is right and what is wrong, but also to demonstrate what we believe to be a *good life*. Both poles cohabit in the contemporary representation of beauty, which today is fiercely associated with health and wellbeing—a good life is one where the body is cared for by medicine, exercise, rigorous diets, and all the available forms of therapy, and is not only right, but also comforting. This is the recipe for wellbeing and happiness promoted by *fitstagrammers*, health bloggers, etc. It's a peculiar combination of a hard-lived and sacrificed life but, at the same time, a pleasant one. Or at least that's what we're told.

Although this might sound convincing up to this point, the most important details are yet to come. Ethical beauty standards come with setbacks. If you fail to meet them, there will be consequences. The paradigm of a *good* life is molded on the image of a *bad* life and, not only that, choosing a bad life is the responsibility of the woman who leads it, as if this was a purely autonomous decision. That leads to labelling women as fat, old-looking (or in fact old), careless, lazy, those who "cannot

control themselves," those who do not take ownership of themselves, those who treat their bodies as a trash can rather than "as
a temple." Before beauty became an ethical ideal, we spoke of
women who were either beautiful or ugly, but we rarely referred
to this as a responsibility. In the novels of the nineteenth century that I love the most, the protagonists are often described
as unattractive. Jo from *Little Women* by Louisa May Alcott,
Jane from *Jane Eyre* by Charlotte Brontë, and Fanny Price from
*Mansfield Park* by Jane Austen, just to name a few, are ungra-
cious (and perhaps it's no coincidence that unattractive heroines abound in literature written by women but are scarce in
literature written by men during the same time). This "short-
coming" is often noticed by the characters that share their
pages (an evil aunt might even mention it to the room), but it's
never considered a moral flaw or, even less so, something they
are guilty of. In our times, conversely, an unattractive woman
is one who let herself go, one who doesn't look after herself,
one who doesn't value herself. It's no longer acceptable to criticize another woman for her appearance, but the intersection of
the discourse of self-love and that of health and wellbeing finds
ways of doing so: it pushes you to love and take care of yourself.
It suggests that you take ownership of your own life and in a
wonderful combination of messages, it might even invite you
to empower yourself, as if giving up carbohydrates or spending
your hard-earned money on an anti-aging face cream was preferable to spending it on having a beer with your friends (or ten
rather, if we consider the cost of an anti-aging face cream).

Laura Contrera and Nicolás Cuello, faces of the fat acceptance movement in Argentina, highlight the morality of thin-
ness as self-control with their concept of *neoliberalismo magro*
[lean neoliberalism].[6] Alluding to a comment made by the former Minister of Economy of Argentina, Alfonso Prat-Gay, on
how to end "fat militancy," Contrera and Cuello highlight how
fat bodies are associated with unproductive corporality, and are

therefore considered inconvenient and of no use. They also categorize these as the bodies of low-income societies (having a thin and toned body is expensive) who are also prone to squandering: on top of being poor they have the insolence to overindulge. As Contrera and Cuello unveil the classicist component of fatphobia, they also expose the moral value that our society attributes to being thin in political terms: a fat person doesn't come across as capable of being part of the public office nor of doing an interview. "If he can't even look after himself, how could he take care of anything else?"

In the twenty-first century, being pretty is not a question of fate; it is a matter of merit. You're either rewarded if you fit in or punished if not. With so much technology and information available, what excuse do we have for not being beautiful? None. If it bothers you that your clothes don't fit, that the male gaze is educated to avoid you, that people laugh at you, humiliate you, or do not take you seriously, you'd better get to work and do your homework. And this is what many of us do, to the best of our abilities. We go to the gym, we read food labels, we buy creams, we research treatments that we can't afford but that seemingly offer the secret of the body we must all learn. We invest time, effort, and money—none of which we have much of—in things that exhaust us. But the guilt is never exhausted, you are never doing enough, you always have a few extra kilograms, spots, open pores, wrinkles, or stretch marks to tackle.

I sometimes ask myself if the girls who closely align with today's beauty ideals truly lead a more carefree life. However, from the times I've had the chance to speak with models due to my work, I certainly didn't get that impression. They live under a huge amount of demoralizing pressure and scrutiny as they struggle to maintain the conditions of their source of work. Being beautiful is a full-time job that—unlike a college career for example, where after a certain number of years you receive a degree upon completion—has no end in sight. And it doesn't become easier with time; on the contrary, with every year that passes, your body requires more work if you want to continue in the race.

We know that men waste less energy and resources on this than we do; that the hours we devote to lymphatic massages or waxing they spend doing something else, something productive or enjoyable, or simply doing nothing—lying down watching television. We know that in theory we could do the same and give up, but the price to pay would be too high. While these are the rules, breaking our backs to look young, thin, firm, and smooth (the four pillars of the contemporary ideal, as Widdows explains) will still be the logical option.

In my research on anorexia nervosa within Orthodox Jewish communities, I came across a study from Toronto that shows that the incidence of this pathology is higher in this community than in the general population in that city. [7] Although in Argentina there are no studies that focus on these communities, the anecdotal evidence that my mother, my sisters, and I have witnessed tells us that this is also a significant problem in Buenos Aires. We understand eating disorders to be complex phenomena that are not related solely to hegemonic beauty standards, but I cannot ignore the perverse logic of the system: prettier girls find the best husbands and hence have access to the best houses, the best clothes, the most comfortable lives. A good marriage is the only possible way to progress socially for an Orthodox girl. Engagements last only a couple of months and impose a great number of limitations, hence first impressions are valuable and, as women have to cover themselves up to their elbows and knees, the only resources available to seduce a man are extremely tight clothes to show a good silhouette and a pretty face (I haven't seen many rhinoplasties in the neighborhood, but the matchmakers of communities in the United States often recommend this as a basic requirement).

When my mother tells me that a young woman that we know is suffering from an eating disorder, I always ask her: "How could you convince her that being thin is not worth ruining her life for when her life depends on it?" In the secular world, this might not be as pronounced, but it's still challenging. On one page of a magazine, we tell young readers that "what matters is within" (within what? Important to whom? Is it, once again, to make us desirable to men?), while on the other pages, we show them pictures of happiness. There's also a clear lack of diverse bodies which, at most, only feature for the sake of "inclusivity" but never as objects of desire. In one of these two cases we are lying to them. "I love myself and my body," a friend of mine tells me, who identifies as fat, "but the world doesn't love it, men don't love it, the people on the streets don't love it. What can I do?"

And I don't know what she can do. Heather Widdows alludes to an idea of responsibility that I somewhat share: If I participate in this race, if I opt for mesotherapy treatments and post my flawless face on Instagram, and if all women do the same, then these will be the only representations of femininity in circulation. This reminds me of the discussion around LGBTQI+ visibility: it's necessary that diverse bodies are shown and seen, and not hidden. In a visual society such as ours, what is not seen does not exist, and what does not exist is not a viable life choice nor an object of desire. People who are labelled fat, wrinkled, old, aged, or who are outside of the narrow margins of what is socially understood as "beautiful people" (also including people with different capabilities) never appear sexualized in public images. They are frequently infantilized, and their sexuality can even be portrayed as a cause of disgust or laughter—those who say that it's a coincidence, or worse "natural" for such bodies to be "disliked" seem to forget that they are very rarely shown as desirable or eroticized. They also ignore the fact that, behind closed doors, people's desire is much more diverse and complex than what is normally depicted. Cherry Vecchio, fat acceptance activist and sex worker, often discusses at events or on her social media that she has encountered many men who specifically look for "fat prostitutes," although in their public lives they never show themselves to be with any women who might be called fat. The age range of the so-called MILFs, including women of over thirty-five or forty years of age (what show business considers "old") is the most popular category searched on almost any porn site.[8] In a society that ceaselessly produces images of sex yet only deems a narrow spectrum of desires acceptable, desiring a body that is considered fat or old is characterized as a fetish or even a kink. This is why fat activism is so valuable, not only for the women who practice it, but also for all of us who are watching: all men and women who are getting used to the idea that bodies that are not thin and smooth as apples have nothing to conceal, that they are as possible and as acceptable as all the other bodies.

Having a body that is relatively accepted by hegemonic beauty standards is a privilege, and renouncing privileges is always difficult. Like the girl at that feminist meeting, I also want others to start. I'm not brave enough to become the heroine of visibility. I don't upload pictures to my social media where I don't look thin or where my neck lines show. Refusing to follow expectations can also be freeing, but let's be realistic: what I say or do will not change anyone's life. What must change are the rules of the game. It's not enough for us to stop playing, although I try to do my part for my own good and as a contribution to general wellbeing. I also try to be aware of the place I occupy—understanding my privilege of belonging to the middle class, of being someone who can afford to go to the gym and choose what to eat, and being thin for whatever reason. This awareness comes to the forefront when I notice that in a writer's group I attend there are no fat women, or that women who are older than me (I do not know if I will ever be fat, but if everything goes well, I will certainly be old) are de-sexualized and considered boring or referred to as Miss.

I also think that there are many blind spots and countless possible paths leading us towards them: girls who love sports and dancing; girls who advocate for a more joyful and positive relationship between women and their bodies or those who encourage us to cherish time with friends over rigorous gym routines. These girls are also changing the world. I exercise because it helps my back and because I must compensate for the hours I spend sitting down writing in front of a screen, but writing has also saved me from having a terrible relationship with the mirror. When I discovered that I cared more about being good at what I did than about looking beautiful, something clicked. "Choosing a diamond-tip microdermabrasion over staying home and reading is never worth it," I constantly remind myself. Today, it's a privilege to dare to dream of something other than being thin and desirable. Those fortunate enough to have access to political, economic, and social resources are free to envision broader dreams for themselves, dreams that are no longer forbidden. It's a privilege to dream of taking political stands, creating art, constructing buildings, writing novels, backpacking around the world, and experiencing sexual adventures or unbelievable romances. Moreover, it's a privilege to envision collective endeavors, communal projects, and forms of happiness that aren't solely individualistic. This is what we should fill the world with: stories of women who do not love or hate their bodies but accept them as they are; of women who are free, truly free, to talk about other things.

# CHAPTER 7
## CONSENT CULTURE

Most of my friends from secular high school came from non-religious families; they celebrated Christmas (or Passover if they came from Jewish homes), but generally, they grew up indifferent to religion. Except for those who—due to their parents' conviction or because they lived nearby—had attended Catholic elementary schools.

I always listened intently to their stories, trying to grasp the rules of their universe. I had a feeling at the time that the sexual morality of Orthodox Jews in Buenos Aires was stricter but easier to understand than the Catholic one. In my community, from the age of twelve you were not allowed to have any contact with men, in the most literal sense possible: we would never greet each other with a kiss, we couldn't play any games that involved any form of touching, we didn't shake hands. It was like that until marriage. There is no hugging, no caressing, no kissing in Orthodox Jewish relationships. I never questioned it until I discovered how things were elsewhere. Now, if I ever (rarely) go to an Orthodox wedding, I can't contain a smile when they show videos with pictures of the couple standing side by side without touching, smiling at the camera as if they were strangers. My friends from elementary school and I didn't speak of "not losing our virginity before marriage." When you can't kiss on the cheek, sex is not a point of discussion, there's no point even mentioning it. When I joined secular high school, I didn't know how common it was to have sex before marriage outside of my community. Only when I was in sixth grade did

I first discuss this with a girl whose cousins were not religious, though she of course didn't know anything about their sexual lives. Our conclusion was that it must be a lot less common than what we saw on television. "Surely they go to bed together once they become engaged," she suggested, "because when they're about to get married it's almost as if they were already married, so they can sleep together then."

On the other hand, Catholic girls, as described by my high school and university friends, inhabited a world made up of constant temptation. Physical contact was not prohibited as it was for us. They greeted each other with a kiss, they hugged their friends, they even danced with boys at parties—though the Sisters took every opportunity to remind them that there was a limit and that crossing it would cost them. Penetration—forbidden—almost became a fetish, an obsession. I was told that within certain groups of friends, the predominant approach was to do "everything except for that." Oral sex, and even anal sex, was a possibility as long as you could preserve your "virginity." "I thought this was nonsense," a girl who had attended a convent school once told me, "because my mother had told me that, aside from virginity, purity was in the heart." Though they were equivalent on a moral level, it was not as clear how one could preserve or lose the purity of the heart.

The Catholic girls that I know are, like I am, "formerly" religious at least in relation to the restrictive sexual morals they learned at a young age (although many of them gave new meaning to their beliefs and religious practice). For years now, they've been living in a world where the question of celibacy before marriage doesn't exist and the restrictions, though they exist, are less strict than those they learned at school. Many of them, like I am, are women's rights activists: we often speak of our sexual education (or rather the complete lack of it) and of what we want for future generations. I believe that we all share a desire for a sexual education that discusses and considers pleasure. Talking about female desire is key when educating men and women to be free and giving them the tools to identify, report, and survive sexual violence. We believe that a world in which a woman is the owner of her own pleasure is a better world. But we don't think it will be easy to build. We've never experienced such a world and don't really know what it could look like; but we are learning what living in such a world would mean. We're still debating what it would mean; it's an ongoing discussion. We're also unsure of the best strategies to achieve this; we're following a trial-and-error method in the only laboratory we have: real life. We know that it will be painful and will pose uncomfortable questions, but we are certain that it will be worth it. After all, we're no strangers to discomfort, especially when discussing our desires.

We're fighting for the right to desire not because it's easy or comfortable, but because we can't—and don't want to—live any other way. Many people speak of times when everything was simpler; in general, I believe that only those who lived through the golden ages or privileged times can think this way. However, they might be right about one thing: when I lived in a universe in which everything was forbidden, I didn't have a good time, but the rules were simple. We didn't find ourselves faced with the dilemmas that complicated the lives of Catholic girls, or those we discuss today with my fellow activists at feminist meetings. When everything is forbidden, there are no grey areas, there's no doubt, no subtlety; there's only room for what is right and what is wrong, the difference is clear and the authorities that delimit where each activity lies, are also clear. The world we are building is different. It will be better, and it will be more complex. But we will use our bodies to tackle that complexity that characterizes freedom.

"We are moved by desire" is one of my favorite mottoes out of the ones that are circulating among feminist groups in

Argentina; I like it because it paves a path that is different to that of retaliation (which is an understandable reaction though not constructive in political and social terms, that is to say when relating to relationships between men, women and non-binary people). It's also different to the path that demands "protection," one that infantilizes us and that—by trapping us in crystal boxes—re-victimizes and blames us for the horror that our bodies and psyche have to go through. In reality, nothing simply happens; there is always a perpetrator who is responsible, in every sense of the word, for these atrocities.

Sohaila Abdulali, journalist and gang rape survivor from India, tells her story in her book *What We Talk about when We Talk about Rape*. In the summer of 1980, when she was seventeen years old, Abdulali went out at night with her male friend in Bombay, as the city was then known. Four men forced them to go up a sand dune, beat them up, raped her, and threatened to castrate him and killing them both if she continued to resist, before finally letting them go after they promised not to report them.

What Abdulali experienced is the quintessential image that many have of rape (an attack by armed, unknown men in the dead of night), and what Rita Segato calls "a gory rape."[1] It is assumed that this type of rape leaves no room for questioning or doubt, unlike the rape cases that occur within relationships (the latter have only recently been recognized as rape, and they remain a "contradiction" for many). But even these cases are faced with skepticism, doubt, mistrust, and enforced silence. The police didn't believe Abdulali and her friend's story, despite the visible injuries they both had. If someone were to go to that police station today to search the records, the only document they would find is a report, signed by her, stating that nothing happened. Sohaila Abdulali lied, but not about having been raped, she lied about *not* having been raped. The police did all they could to stop her from reporting the crime. But as she insisted, they told her that if she reported the incident, she would be kept under custody in Bombay supposedly "for her own protection." Abdulali had just been accepted to a university in the United States and staying there would have prevented her from starting her course. The criminal justice system (particularly those policemen, who would rather not stain the reputation of their district with a rape case) put her in a difficult position: that of choosing between telling the story of what had happened to her or living the life she had chosen for herself. Abdulali did not hesitate.

She eventually told her truth, first in a journalistic article and then in her book, but this was not easy. India's left-wing politics of the time, she explains, only left room for discussing rape that happened in the context of the oppression of class and race. "Privileged" women like her, who did not fit into that narrative, had no place in such a conversation. And, in subjective terms, Abdulali felt cornered by the trap that sexual violence victims still face today: talking about the fact that she had been raped turned her into a victim, someone deserving of compassion and protection (again). She didn't like that image, nor did she feel it suited her, but on the other hand if she wasn't a victim, if she had not been completely broken, what was she complaining about? If she had managed to keep it together, could she be lying or at least exaggerating? Was she a crybaby, repeatedly complaining? Was she being capricious and seeking attention? Those were—and still are—the spaces available in the collective mind for women who survive sexual violence. The woman who decides to speak of what was done to her must be willing to accept one of these labels.

Up until recently, Abdulali would often cite two feminist concepts against sexual violence that she now considers to be problematic: "*No* means *no*, and *yes* means *yes*," on one hand, and on the other the idea that rape has nothing to do with sex and that it's only related to power. "Now I realize," she wrote in 2018, "sometimes *yes* doesn't mean *yes*, and sometimes rape *does* have to do with sex."[2]

This is what we mean when we talk of rape culture.[3] That not all men are rapists, not every case of abuse or harassment is equivalent to rape, and that having been sexist once does not warrant public shaming or criminal punishment. Audre Lorde said it once: "The master's tools will never dismantle the master's house."[4] Besides, we've all been sexist at some point (and we still are to a certain extent). In the most recent wave of feminism in Argentina, the term "deconstruction," coined by French philosopher Jacques Derrida, gained significant popularity. "Deconstruction" primarily refers to questioning gender mandates. While philosophical concepts often evolve and sometimes become almost unrecognizable over time, this transformation doesn't concern me. I suspect Derrida, who himself challenged the idea of fixed meanings, might have felt the same. But I believe there is a nuance in the idea of deconstruction as he introduced it that would be interesting to return to. In *Force of Law: The Mystical Foundation of Authority*[5] he references the nature of justice as both impossible and necessary: justice—in a metaphysical rather than criminal sense, though this idea can be applied to challenge criminal justice too—always comes too late and attempts to correct what cannot be corrected and repair the irreparable. But, at the same time, we feel compelled to seek justice and even feel responsible to do so. Can something impossible be at the same time so essential? That is precisely the issue, the paradox. Deconstruction doesn't offer a clear system of values dictating what should or shouldn't be done; it does not separate the good from the bad, and even less so good people from bad people. It's always an imperfect view, it isn't all-encompassing, it doesn't decide on a specific option because it's the best one according to an irrefutable parameter but because making decisions is always an urgency. We cannot stop the world from turning until we know what to do afterwards; we must continue living and making mistakes and waiting to see what stems from those failed decisions. We are condemned to live in a permanent draft that's continually being re-written.

We will not stop having sex until we can deconstruct rape culture. And none of us—men or women—are "safe," "outside" or "above" this. It is not about affirming that you are on the "right side" (as it is the terrible case of the men who flaunt their supposed deconstruction until they become the parody of themselves). Nor is it about saying "I understand that some people are worried, I don't need to reconsider anything because I was always a feminist" (I've read this phrase in various magazines); of course it's not about holding our hands up in self-flagellation and self-denigration. The deconstructive view proposes an undoing of our own practices, a reckoning of our most cherished bonds and of our most deeply rooted convictions. We must not do it thinking that we're "solving a problem," that we'll find a solution, that we'll know what we must do. Deconstruction is the need to continue a conversation that has no conclusion.

When I was ten years old, I became obsessed with television, particularly with series and soaps. They were the window to life on the outside of my bubble, so as well as watching them, I spent hours staring at the ceiling, reflecting on what I had watched: a kiss, a conversation, an argument between the protagonist and her mother. I did not distinguish between fictional promises, tones, or geographies. The most implausible melodramas, where girls would lose their sight or the functionality of their legs and then regained them in the next episode—like *La usurpadora*, *Esmeralda*, *Topacio*, made for Latin American women—began to get mixed up in my head with the American teen series I could watch on cable (*Dawson's Creek*, *Beverly Hills 90210*, *Gilmore Girls*, just to mention the first three that come to mind).

A detailed analysis of these series and soaps would find a great number of differences between them. However, at the time, I was looking for common patterns, and one of the most evident was the idea that sex was a gift women used to negotiate or to keep rather than a form of pleasure. When Abdulali writes that often rape has nothing to do with sex, she is talking about this. That the sex we have (and frequently the sex we *almost* have) is infused with notions that legitimize and feed unequal and even violent gender dynamics. An evident case is the idea that sex is something that men demand and that women concede to. Rape culture is present in different practices and discourses that do not appear to be violent on surface level.

In these soaps, sex was disgraceful and shameful; something the "villains" did to divert a handsome man from the path of pure and angelical simplicity that would lead him to the heroine. Other television series pretended to be liberal, but they did the same. Brenda Walsh, Rory Gilmore, Joey Potter, and other female protagonists rarely thought of having sex; instead, the subject only appeared in a scene as a demand from a man. And not any man; always the boyfriend who had gained enough merit to be deserving of this concession. According to the script, sex did not spark any kind of desire or even curiosity in its female characters; it only generated anxiety and fear. However, as I lay face down in my bedroom in Balvanera, it intrigued me, and the fact that it was so feared by the girls on TV raised many questions in me. Was having sex such a serious, important matter? Did "losing your virginity" change your life? Why was it only life-changing for women and not for men? If television depicted it as such a horrific and dangerous activity, why do all women end up doing it anyway? What was the good part?

Above everything else, this is what was missing from the point of view of women. Someone who spoke of the good part of sex, of why enjoyment was a possibility. The only valuable aspect of sex for a woman that I could deduce from watching television was its exchange value: sex was something men wanted and giving it to them could secure their love. But the exchange was not so simple. Because if it were, the girls who had more sex would be the most loved ones, and that not only did not happen, but television also endeavored to communicate that the opposite could happen to them. Each pure and sweet heroine had a counterfigure, the mean and promiscuous girl who no one could "truly" love (though she was easily accepted in other interactions on a daily basis). Even series aimed at a young audience, which explored the theme in a more subtle way, never presented a promiscuous girl as the heroine. There was always "the other one," an extreme example against whom the protagonist could measure herself and ensure that her sexuality was under control.

"Third date: one more than a slut and one less than a puritan," says Carrie Bradshaw, protagonist of *Sex and the City* (a series which, classism and all, was among the best ones in terms of sexual freedom), referring to the perfect moment to have sex with a man. I must have been ten years old the first time I heard this, but the phrase still stuck with me. I believed it condensed everything I needed to know about "sex." Being a slut was wrong, but being a nun was also wrong: you had to hit the sweet spot of desire, but how to find it? That's what I put into practice during the following years. That's how I learned that the benchmark was set by male desire. Having sex when they wanted to, how they wanted to, with whoever they wanted to have sex with; no more, no less.

While *no* always means *no*, there are times when *yes* is more ambiguous precisely because the way we have learned to have sex is tainted with a complex ideology and stems from a culture in which female desire is a taboo rather than a subject. That is rape culture: to be able to say *yes* or *no*, we must be able to talk about sex, think about sex, and put a name to our feelings. We cannot protest nor avoid what cannot be said, but we can suffer from it.

María del Mar Ramón, a Colombian feminist of my generation who lives in Argentina, wrote a piece titled "Fucking without wanting to and without saying no (the history of consent)"[6] in which she discusses this topic. Although it was published in a magazine from Guatemala, many Argentinian women read it and said that they recognized themselves in her story and that reading it had helped them think about the limits of what we understand as consent: "a *yes* is a *yes*, and a *no* is a *no*." María's story isn't a gory nor a terrible one: it's a story of mediocre sex. She meets a man that she likes in a bar, she does feel like having sex with him but not at the exact same moment that he wants to have sex with her. He's perhaps a step ahead of her. He becomes insistent and because she wants him to like her, she gives in after initially hesitating. She's not comfortable, she's not having a good time: she tries to show this in many ways, but she never expresses it explicitly. She says nothing. In the end, she leaves after having had mediocre sex. He loses interest and his good manners. María del Mar asks herself what happened. "I would've liked to feel something other than discomfort all night long. I would've liked to have been governed by consent rather than resignation," she writes. "It was a terrible night, I think. Another one. Nights like this are not uncommon and at least nothing 'serious' happened. I feel slightly uncomfortable and uneasy, and I can't distract myself with another thought that would help me forget. What happened was something that I did not want to happen, but I couldn't say that I didn't want it. It wasn't that man's fault, but it certainly wasn't my fault either."

In a situation like this, there's no point in trying to find the guilty party. Instead we should ask ourselves what went wrong. Why did María del Mar not say anything? Why did she not feel that there was room to say *no* or *not now*, *later*, or *not this way*? Why did he not notice? Did he not want to notice, or did he pretend not to notice? That man is not a rapist, but *that* is rape culture. He learned that success on a night out depends on whether he has sex or not and in that race, the woman's pleasure becomes secondary; she learned that men have to be pleased, that maintaining their attention is more important than having a good time, and that there are certain things that are better left unsaid to avoid seeming needy and ruining the atmosphere of such a wonderful night (not so wonderful for her, and perhaps deep down not wonderful for him either, but that's irrelevant). This is why, as Abdulali said, in some cases non-consensual sex—or "almost" non-consensual, as uncomfortable as it is to admit it, there are plenty of grey areas in these situations—has a lot to do not only with power, but also with sexual education and the roles it teaches men and women to embody.

Many women have similar anecdotes to share. I have one. When I was fifteen years old, the boy I lost my virginity to and I—I would have said boyfriend at the time, but today I'm certain that he wasn't—had been trying to plan my first time, but something always got in the way: either plans failed, or something didn't quite work out. He had begun to get bored, and I also felt frustrated, but neither of us had said how we felt. A couple of nights later, we planned to go dancing with my friends and his. We all met up at his place and at one point, with everyone around, he asked me to help him with something in his bedroom. We began to try to have sex again, though I didn't feel like it. I already felt anxious enough about it, I didn't need to add to it ten people behind the door. Like María del Mar, I tried to show him with my body that I was not sure about what was happening, that I was uncomfortable, that I wasn't having a good time, but he had decided to get this over and done with, and at a certain point I began to think that it was a good idea too. We got dressed and returned to the group without saying a word.

When we arrived at the nightclub there was a long line. I

told my friends that I didn't want to wait that long; he stayed with his friends. We'd only been going out for a couple of months but after that night we never spoke again. We didn't "break up," we simply stopped calling each other. At the time I assumed that he had grown tired of my clumsiness, of my lack of experience, and lack of sensuality. I'm not ruling these possibilities out, but the distance of time has led me to think that there could be another possibility: he was partially conscious that what had happened was wrong, but he didn't know why, nor how to apologize. I was also confused, I felt upset and angry, but I didn't understand what or who made me feel that way, nor how I could have had a conversation about it. There was no vocabulary to name what had happened to us; the only thing we had been taught about that uncomfortable boundary between sex and violence was that it was better not to discuss it.

We will never know what the men in María del Mar's story or mine would have done had we voiced our no; we will never know what we would have done if, instead of carrying on with something that we clearly were not completely enjoying, they had asked us if we were having a good time. What we do know is that our stories are not isolated incidents. In Latin America, according to a report presented by Oxfam in 2018, "eighty-seven percent of young men and women aged between fifteen and twenty-five believed that men have greater sexual desire than women. This portrays women as incapable of feeling either desire or pleasure, and firmly establishes their enjoyment as secondary to a man's desires."[7]

According to this report, sixty-five percent of men aged between fifteen and nineteen agree with the idea that women say *no* when they mean *yes*. But I believe that María del Mar and I, as well as our respective partners, at least deserved to receive sexual education that would have enabled us to speak about what we desired as well as to listen—in the broadest sense of the word—to the other's desire. We deserved to learn how to navigate the complexities of desire without all the veils, taboos, and shame, not only at school but also in general culture, within our families, and with our friends.

I know that the way in which I analyze these stories might be slightly shocking. It might even seem like I'm equating male and female characters, as if having sex with someone when you don't want to and you're trying to make it evident is the same as having sex with someone who—you should know—doesn't want to have sex with you. This is not what I mean, at least not exactly. I chose to discuss Sohaila Abdulali's story, but also two cases of men with whom it is difficult to empathize, precisely because these are the cases that make us the most uncomfortable. Not only because they are difficult to judge, but also because they evidence that non-consensual sex is far from being an exception in our culture, "perverted" behavior, or unanimously repudiated. It overlaps with the way in which most of us learn how to relate to and to think about sex.

I am interested in showing that sexual aggressors don't appear out of thin air. They were also not "born" that way. According to Diana Scully, author of one of the most celebrated reports on sexual violence,[8] rapists *learn* how to rape. And they don't learn it at a secret underground school for rapists, but at the same school and the same institutions where we learn about what being a man supposedly means, which is the exact same learning. They learn the same as the boys and girls who answered the Oxfam survey: that men have hypertrophied sexual impulses that are impossible to control, that this is why they do what they do and, because they cannot control themselves, girls must not complain too much when this happens.

They learn that this selfish and violent way of experiencing sexuality, without considering the other, is not only tolerable, but it is also desirable and even mandatory. To Scully's idea of sex education, Rita Segato adds the concept of rape as a mandate: "this mandate established by society rules in the mental horizon of the sexually violent man by means of interlocutors that lurk in the shadows, who the criminal makes responsible for his actions and through whom he acquires his full meaning," she writes.[9] "And the mandate," Segato continues, "expresses the social precept that the man must be capable of displaying his virility as a component that is indiscernible from masculinity and subjectivity by claiming the female agent as his own [ . . . ]. In other words, the subject rapes not because he has the power to do so or to demonstrate that he does, but because he must obtain it."

This concept of rape as a combination of practices that are taught and learned namely, as a culture—distances itself from the idea that a sexually violent man is "sick," an outlook that prior to Scully's analysis, was the only one available to conceptualize these behaviors. "Rather than examining the case histories of sexually violent men for evidence of pathology [ . . . ] or for individual motives," Scully writes, "I have used convicted rapists collectively as expert informants on a sexually violent culture."[10] In this study, the man who rapes is not considered an "ordinary man," however, he is not considered to be sick or an outcast either. He is an expert in rape culture, he embodies an extreme version of the range of violence that society legally condemns while continuing to feed its practice and subjective structures.

Segato's idea of rape as a mandate adds a key layer of meaning. The man who rapes does not do it because he has power (though in many cases his power does help him prevent the consequences of his actions); he obtains power through this action. The affirmation that rape is not related to sex but to power that Abdulali shares appears then to be both correct and incorrect at the same time. Rape is directly related to power and directly related to sex because the way in which we are taught to think of sex is directly related to the difference between power, drive, and desire— against which we are told we are powerless.

"Boys are like that," generations of fathers, mothers, teachers, and religious figures have said and continue to say. "You must look after yourself, cover up, don't expose yourself; you're to blame for wearing a short skirt and going out at night alone ("alone," in this context, applies to both a single woman and a group of women without a man).

Women also learn that if culture teaches men to "claim women as their own" so that they can become true men, women (feminized identities) are taught the counterpart of this narrative; we learn to tolerate it and even desire it. We learn that a violent man is a sensual one, that this is the exact definition of sex appeal. A man who doesn't take you against your will doesn't desire you enough, a man who isn't jealous doesn't love you enough, a man who doesn't insist doesn't find you attractive enough (and there is no worse tragedy than that).

The space for genuine pleasure, where a woman can boldly pursue her desires, must be consciously cultivated, it must be demanded and fought for in the context of a patriarchal culture that affirms that pleasure is not for you. But the social, political, and discursive space for saying no is also not a given territory, but rather one that we must build collectively. Having the mental space, the true possibility of saying no when we want to, without giving any explanations nor apologizing, has nothing to do with being prudish. It is a feminist conquest.

Towards the end of 2018, actor Thelma Fardín gave a press conference organized by the collective Actrices Argentinas [Argentinian Actors], in which she revealed that she had been raped by actor Juan Darthés when she was sixteen years old, and he was over forty. This happened in Nicaragua during the tour of the Argentine teen drama *Patito Feo* (*Ugly Duckling*), in which Darthés was practically the only adult in the cast. Many years passed, though not enough for such a crime to become statute-barred in Nicaragua. This is why Thelma, assisted by a feminist lawyer, pursued legal action before making the crime public knowledge.

This story sent shockwaves throughout the country. All the prejudices and stereotypes surrounding sexual violence victims suddenly had a face and a name. A lot of people wondered why it had taken Fardín nearly a decade to report Darthés; others delved into her past, searching for photos where she was smiling, taken around the same time as the rape; many others questioned her story without any reason and simply said that "it's one person's word against the other's," or that feminism was going too far. There were also other reactions: women who began to tell their stories, teenagers who discussed sexual violence with their parents for the first time at the dinner table in front of the television, activists and journalists brought the issue to the headlines across all media. And in this turmoil, a discussion that many feminists had been having quietly—within our activist groups, with our friends and classmates, and even with our partners—became public. What do we do in the face of sexual violence? Is criminal punishment the best solution in all the cases? Is public shaming and embarrassment better? Do we want the perpetrators to burn in hell and never be able to set foot on the streets again? Do we want to mark their foreheads as if they had a biblical curse? Do we want to hang the scarlet letter around their necks as they did with adulterous women in New England in the seventeenth century?

While I recognize that criminal justice is often an essential part of the process, I'm also aware of the flaws in the system that can discriminate, oppress, and even torture people. With this in mind, it would be deeply unjust for me to suggest (from the comfort of my laptop) that reporting a crime isn't the solution, especially for women who endure daily abuse from their partners. Derrida's warning in his rationalization of deconstruction has never been more pertinent than in this context: emergencies do not wait for us to have the necessary tools to solve them.

One outcome we must cautiously prevent is that of feminist demands being co-opted by those who fight for increasingly punitive and controlling societies. We are moved by desire and desire must continue to be the goal: we want dissidence, not order. We don't want a committee to define courtship rules or, at least, we cannot want this as feminists. These attempts to regularize or repress come from diverse sectors; there are those who of course want to "lock up all rapists behind bars" (or castrate or kill them) and try to sell that hatred as a contribution to women's campaigns. There are also those who with the best intentions assume that they have found the miraculous formula of consent (the Holy Grail that guarantees the impossibility of misunderstandings, ambiguity, and suffering) but forget that in an activity such as sex, which is teeming with ambiguity, and a risk of being questioned and even harmed, there is no way of opening up without being exposed to potential suffering.

In the United States, universities talk of affirmative consent in an attempt to reduce the countless rapes that happen on their campuses. This posits that a man must obtain explicit consent at every step of the way during the sexual encounter. I believe that there are components of this idea that are valuable: encouraging clear conversations and debunking the prejudice that asking the other what they want is a turn-off[11] are two essential points. However, obsessing about the magic word, about finding a standardized formula for distinguishing violent situations from non-violent ones is futile and can even become counterproductive. I say futile because that magic word does not exist; we know that not even a hyper-explicit "yes," under conditions of vulnerability or inequality, is a straightforward "yes." And I say counterproductive because it depicts sexual violence as a purely technical issue: as if the problem men faced was that of finding a secret and unerring signal that constitutes consent. Sohaila Abdulali addresses men to tell them that it is O.K. to look for logical signals, to proceed cautiously. It's not about magical formulas, but rather about a genuine concern for what is happening to the other person: there are no technicalities that could help a man who has been educated not to look at the woman who stands in front of him. The main concern lies in successfully reeducating, not in compiling a list of unequivocal rules and signals that allow you or forbid you to proceed.

We do not want codes made up by paranoid deans who are merely covering up their own backs so that the university doesn't have to face a trial; we want symbolic and material circumstances that enable a negotiation—with the terms of our choosing—of what we want and do not want to do. We want to be treated as responsible adults with the ability to give consent, to desire, to make decisions, and to recognize those decisions as our own. For this to happen, we need those decisions to be viable options. If my negative response is going to be ignored, there is no point in learning how to verbalize it; if I don't have the means to move out of the house I share with my rapist, emancipation through subjective terms will not be enough.

We don't want revenge either; again, we cannot want revenge if we are feminists. It isn't surprising that many women want those who hurt them to pay for it: because we're humans, forged with the heat of a patriarchal culture that adheres to those terms since—at least—Hammurabi; because we are angry; because we've been brought up with the idea that people must pay for their sins, that "bad people" must get what they deserve, and that this is what justice is. This way of thinking is not only present in the right-wing sectors of Argentina, who call for more strict sentencing and for the age of criminal responsibility to be decreased. It's also present in a form of intervention that has a complex history: public shaming. Public shaming was first used in Argentina as an instrument of popular justice against the impunity that Menemism[12] accorded oppressors who acted during the dictatorship between 1974 and 1983. Public shaming became a way of remembering and of protecting ourselves (singling out a terrible element to avoid being affected by its violence) against a government that attempted to wipe out the horrors caused by the civil-military dictatorship. Two key points always underscored the argument in favor of public shaming: first, that it emerged in a context where the government and its criminal justice system were inactive; and second, that these oppressors had been pardoned for their imprescriptible crimes.

In recent years, the focus of public shaming in Argentina is on accusations made by women who have been sexually abused. Thelma Fardín's case didn't classify as public shaming as, before the public accusation, she had reported the crime to the legal authorities. Instead, it took the shape of public and collective support of a collective of actors and the lawyer Sabrina Cartabia, who stood beside Fardín during the press conference so that she would not be eaten alive by the media when she communicated what she had decided to do.[13] However, the case exposed all the issues surrounding today's popular form of public shaming— on social media, often anonymously—and frequently related to behaviors that do not constitute as crimes in the eye of the law. Speaking out is freeing; naming one's trauma is cathartic. It's a pivotal step in the healing journey for many women, something I've observed firsthand in numerous feminist discussion groups. Having the courage to tell your story, while being surrounded by comrades who are not judging or questioning you is as painful as it is healing; and we must continue to build safe spaces that are not just public conferences where we can have these conversations. I'm not interested in questioning those who have decided to follow the route of public shaming—be it because they wanted to, because it felt good, or because they were tortured by the frustration of the offender not paying for what he had done. The last thing I want to do is blame them for anything. I am interested in asking myself: at which point does public shaming, applied to cases that are not criminal offences, cease to be a politically productive strategy? I think about all those boys who answered Oxfam's survey, the sixty-five percent of boys between the ages of fifteen and nineteen who believe that women mean no when they say yes. I am sure that there are ways to deconstruct discourses, and the habits those discourses generate, but is public shaming an opportunity to learn? "Now that'll teach him," some say. Really? Will it? Can anyone learn anything from public shaming and derision? It's almost as if we were taking "blood, sweat and tears" as a literal punishment. It doesn't strike me as the best way to learn how to better our relationships.

The underlying concept of punishment found in public shaming highlights the importance of calling out a culprit instead of focusing on collective change. Accepting the narrative that places public shaming as the main tool is buying into the idea that, if we mark all the violent men with a cross on their foreheads, we will solve the problem. It also means deciding that we care more about segregating the "good ones" from the "bad ones" rather than looking inward, revisiting our education, beginning to change the way we think, and educating future generations differently. It means accepting that there is no way to eradicate rape culture and that we can only clear the path using machetes. We must continue to speak up and to heal, but instead of encouraging a society driven by punishment and derision, we must direct our political energy towards building something new. I am not speaking (of course!) of turning the other cheek, but rather of what we have started to call consent culture:[14] allowing our desire, rather than resistance, to drive eroticism—that a woman with desires is not "easy" or "a turn-off" (because "if there's no challenge it's no fun"). I'm not suggesting that this is easy, in fact in earlier pages I wrote the opposite of that: a life lived freely is better, but it's perhaps more uncomfortable when the other option is to stay in the structures that we have learned.

The discussion surrounding sexual violence highlights how difficult—perhaps impossible—it is to tackle a systemic problem without changing the whole system. The problem is not just the government or criminal law, capitalist labor relations also thwart egalitarian bonds. I think of the conversations I have with my friends about the companies and universities that we're part of, and how they attempt to prohibit relationships between adults of different hierarchies (in reality universities are not doing much, but professors who are historically famous for going out with their pupils are beginning to be afraid). We don't want a world where it is forbidden to have sex with your boss or your professor if you want to; what we want is a world where, if that desire arises, you do not have to ask yourself what consequences it will have on your academic, professional, or financial life. The same must be said of course if the desire is not present and you have to say no to your boss or professor. How can we achieve this while there are still relations of power and dependence? Can we generate genuine emotional bonds in a world of precarious financial relationships where your survival depends on whether you are liked, whether you smile enough, or whether you make yourself loveable?[15] We will have to look for another way because we cannot forbid people to date someone who earns more than them. We can ask ourselves why it's generally men who look to date subordinates, what form of pleasure they find in that asymmetry (or why there are so many more men in leadership positions). We can also question our own actions; how we have been taught to become loveable and complacent with our superiors. When a compliment comes from a homeless person, society teaches us to be repulsed, yet if it comes from our boss, it is an honor (even if you hate it). We can do this from the cracks present in the system, and while they exist, we hope that the police force is trained in gender perspectives. Nonetheless, we would prefer to have a world without police.

In other words, we must think about the ways in which we navigate these conflicts in the context of capitalism, because that is the system in which we live today and most of us will most likely not witness another one. Without losing sight of the way in which feminism opposes all the inequalities, not only gender ones, we can view a subject that seems to be "localized" as a magnifying glass that helps us find the ways in which unfettered capitalism hurts us, and the watchful government re-victimizes us. There is no code of conduct that can erase the inequality between a domestic worker and her employer; inequality that, furthermore, is protected by the sacred privacy of a bourgeois household. As long as work is a necessity for living, saying no to a man who can give you a job will continue to be a difficult situation.

In the cracks of the patriarchy and capitalism, there lies the potential to build a culture of consent. I don't want to appear to be led by blind optimism, but I believe that consent culture can be explosive and can add wood to a fire that could burn these two structures that govern us. A culture where imposing yourself on a woman and consuming her is no longer worthy of admiration (better yet, one in which this is worthy of disgust); a culture where I can recognize the desires of the person in front of me, regardless of their gender; a culture in which I do not take whatever is given to me because I can or, as the rape mandate would say, because I must and because to establish myself as a male subject I must follow my hyper-desire until it leads me to violence.

This is not impossible. In fact, in Argentina and elsewhere in the world, we're already doing it. By means of inclusive sexual education—something we must protect daily—because, if we let our guard down, it will be taken from us. We will work so that it continues to exist because it is also prevention. At the end of the day, nobody wants to be raped so that they can send their rapist to jail. What we want is not to be raped. To be free, to be peers. For that we must deconstruct, but we must also create: this new civilization that we are creating (I'd rather not say "giving birth to") comes from our political imagination, but not exclusively. It comes from our whole bodies. We are moved by frustration, we are moved by pain but, most of all, we are moved by desire.

I was going to write that we all have an opinion on maternity, but the truth is that what we have are questions, and not only those of us who aren't mothers: many women who already have children don't know why they decided to have them. Some are not even sure if they did "decide": they say that it isn't a decision in the traditional sense of the word but rather a combination of decisions—taken in a certain context and under certain circumstances—and something else, though they can't quite say what.

My friends who are around forty years old say that the conversational focus eventually shifts, that it's characteristic of our age: that afterwards the one who had children did, and the others simply did not, and no one discusses the subject anymore. My mother and other women of her generation, raised in the sixties, tell me that they didn't debate this because having children was a given. Even those who did not have them can't remember having conversations about it, or a specific moment in which they decided not to have children. "It just didn't happen," they say with the conviction that, if they had wanted to, one way or another, they would have had them.

Millennials speak about this subject regularly because we're reaching the age in which—by societal standards—women are expected to have children, but also because we are living in a time that has an extremely peculiar relationship with maternity. On the one hand, my mother and her friends say that having children is not an obvious choice anymore. A certainty only very few women used to move away from is today a question, an insidious and difficult question. So difficult that some of my friends frequently say (and what would be the point in lying, I do too) that they would like to not have to make that decision, to just accidentally become pregnant or find out that they can't have children; let our bodies decide for us. Even these options—we uphold from our privilege of being able to afford birth control methods and even abortions if necessary—seem preferable to the anguish of having to take responsibility for such a crucial decision.

There is a sense that the requirements on mothers are becoming increasingly demanding. Requirements coming from the media, from books for "new moms", and from social media. Women receive endless directives on what they must and must not do to become good mothers. Feeding their babies with a bottle rather than breastfeeding, letting their child watch television for a short while, allowing them to eat French fries, or making them sleep in their own room—all relatively commonplace behaviors when I was a child—are now mortal sins. Those who don't want to or can't comply with all these rules live a life full of guilt and shame. You only have to click on an online forum to find women who don't have the option not to return to work after three months of paid maternity leave (what is granted in Argentina) and are despairing because, according to the information they've found, a baby who is fed with a bottle is doomed to become a psychopath. In addition, this return to the fifties did not come, at least in Argentina, with state policies that allow all women to practice motherhood in this way. We're caught in a paradox: full dedication to one's baby is viewed as a moral obligation, yet it isn't universally recognized as a right.

As I think of what my fate will be, I wonder whether these two seemingly contradictory currents are not in reality two sides of the same coin. Is there a correlation between the revival of full-time motherhood—one that stigmatizes women who choose or are conditioned by class to have a role of working mothers—and the fact that an increasing number of women are allowing themselves to think that a life without children is a tangible option? Does the notion of women without children unsettle societal norms? Is there something disquieting about women who might want children but still want to see themselves in different roles, in places other than their homes, their kitchens, and their baby's room? Is there something alarming about women who dare to be greedy enough to desire something other than giving themselves completely to another? And going back to the girls in the online forum, what about a woman who would like to dedicate her life to being a mother rather than working but can't, yet still has the audacity to become pregnant? The prevailing norm that suppresses a woman's desire—be it the desire to be a mother or the desire not to be a mother—seems to be the undeniable truth of today.

It's interesting, as noted by Chilean writer Lina Meruane in her book of essays *Contra los hijos* (*Against Children*), that Virginia Woolf did not include children among the female obligations listed in her speech "Professions for Women." The "duty of motherhood" is left out of the list of domestic obligations that, as Woolf explains to an auditorium of young women, conspire against her professional development. Why? "Perhaps she is afraid of warning young, professional women about a social imposition against working mothers, perhaps she is afraid of making them doubt their professional drive, their ambitions,"[1] Meruane considers. This is an interesting position; however, my intuition takes me elsewhere. The mandate of maternity is, at its core, different from other norms that dictate what it means to be a good housewife. Cleaning, sweeping the floors, and ironing are all tasks that almost anyone can recognize as customary, boring, and inconsequential; in fact, since time immemorial, privileged women have delegated these tasks to poorer women without diminishing their standing in the eyes of the patriarchy. Those who don't hire domestic help are still grateful for inventions such as the washing machine and the microwave. It's understood that no one truly "loves" cleaning oil stains or defrosting chicken, which are tasks that have a value of their own but the less time one spends on them the better (which is partly the reason why labor characterized as female is not even recognized as such: because no one else would want to do it, but someone has to, given that these tasks are as tedious as they are essential).

The same cannot be said for motherhood. Feminists of all traditions have spoken about procreation as the norm, but even those who—like Simone de Beauvoir or Shulamith Firestone—defended their personal decision of not having children, left room for thinking that other women could want them. Polishing floors is no one's deep-rooted desire, but motherhood can be for many people. I believe this to be one of the greatest philosophical difficulties when thinking about motherhood: the fact that in a single word, in a single idea, two ways of living as contradictory as mandate and desire can cohabit.

Adrienne Rich was the first one to put this issue into clear words: "I try to distinguish," she writes in *Of Woman Born: Motherhood as Experience and Institution*, "between two meanings of motherhood, one superimposed on the other: the potential relationship of any woman to her powers of reproduction and to children; and the institution, which aims at ensuring that that potential—and all women—shall remain under male control."[2] Rich hopes to be able to clearly separate these two extremes. She knows that to achieve this separation, the profound influence of motherhood, as an institution on women's lives, must be acknowledged.

Historically, being a mother was a question of fate rather than a choice. Not only for biological reasons (we often forget that the pill, the first reliable contraceptive method for women that requires no collaboration from the male counterpart, is less than one hundred years old) but also social. Our grandmothers did not have the contraceptive pill, but many had abortions: they had them illegally and risked their lives. They were frequently accompanied by other women, though others did it alone. Some men surely supported them but, judging by the stories I've heard from older women, this was extremely rare. "Our husbands knew, they weren't stupid," a woman over eighty years old explained at a conference I attended, "but they pretended they didn't. They didn't agree or disagree. They thought it was our business." The point is that, still today, deciding whether to become a mother or not is not a possibility for many women, this was even truer in the past. And this is because we don't speak of the fact that many women who give birth against their will were also penetrated against their will. "If rape has been terrorism," writes Rich, "motherhood has been penal servitude. *It need not be*,"[3] she adds. This statement summarizes it perfectly: can motherhood be different to what we have been taught about it? Can it not be enslaving, alienating, disempowering for women? What is missing for it not to be?

In my mind, the concept of motherhood as a mandate (what Rich calls *institution*) is a lot more concrete than the opposing concept of motherhood as a desire (what Rich calls *experience* relating to possibility). In Orthodox Judaism, the idea that young girls are raised to become mothers is a literal one: girls don't *just* play with dolls and strollers or *just* receive kitchens as a gift. Strictly speaking, I don't remember my primary school friends owning kitchen toys because, in Once, "playing at cooking" meant helping your mother in the kitchen. My situation was an exceptional one because my mother had a job and, as she became a widow very young, she "only" had three daughters; but most of the girls from my neighborhood shared their houses with a minimum of five or six siblings, and all daughters were expected to contribute with household duties as well as with looking after the smaller siblings. Leaving a thirteen year-old girl in charge of her younger siblings seemed crazy to my friends from the secular world, but in the neighborhood this was ordinary.[4] And it wasn't only done out of necessity or to alleviate the mother's duties, it was believed that girls had to begin practicing early to be prepared for when their turn would come to become mothers, which is not something too distant when you are thirteen years old—the ideal scenario was getting married as soon as you finished high school and, by the time you reached twenty-two years old, expecting your second or third child.

When I was in sixth grade, we had a subject called "traditions for women" (*Dinim labat*, in Hebrew) while the boys learned how to interpret the Talmud. We learned tasks such as cleaning lettuce to get rid of the insects so that, in a couple of years, we could make sure that our family's food was *kosher*.

Motherhood presented itself to me at a young age as the future my friends were destined for, and the future I had to escape from at all costs. If someone had asked me, I would have said that I did imagine myself having children but "when I was much older." Only recently did I understand just how much the idea of motherhood as fate had become engrained in my subconscious. I guess that's why, now I've reached the "much older" age I referred to back then, motherhood still feels like a form of slavery to me. I understand, in theory, the concept of motherhood as desire, and I would like that to be my case but if I am honest with myself, it's still too foreign to me.

There's a central paradox in the dichotomy Rich proposes: we're surrounded by messages about motherhood, but they're rarely related to desire. Motherhood can appear as a punishment for desiring too much or as the price to pay for wanting to have sex; this was the message repeatedly used in 2018 by those who criticized the legalization of abortion in Argentina. Another prevalent narrative that stems from common sense is that of "being fulfilled as a woman," of "growing up." In fact, many cultures see motherhood as the true rite of passage into adulthood. I can confirm this is the case in Orthodox Judaism, and I don't believe things outside of this community to be very different, at least in Argentina and Latin America: hence the myth that people who don't want to have children suffer from the "Peter Pan complex" as they wish to remain children eternally.

I've also heard statements such as "all women want children" or "all women want to have that experience." These conceptions use the same words Adrienne Rich used to describe the idea of motherhood as an experience, only in reverse. Desire is in principle multiform and not a certainty. We aren't born with it, we don't inherit it, we don't have it simply because we're women—biologically or not. Desire is, in its essence, volatile and diverse: we cannot all want the same. If we don't make space for that multiplicity without caring about the word we use for it, we aren't speaking of desire or using the concept in the right way. And if we say that women's desire is to be mothers because it's their destiny or because it is their duty, we are entering the territory of contradiction, as desire has absolutely nothing to do with duty and obligations.

It also has nothing to do with instrumental and practical rationality. One does not desire because it's "convenient" or logical. Perhaps it's more difficult to think about it in relation to sexual desire. We might think it strange if, for example, after telling a friend we want to sleep with a man, she were to ask: "why?" Maybe because I want to? However, those are not easily accepted reasons for wanting or not wanting to be a mother if the patriarchy judges the circumstances to be inadequate.

On the flip side, many who, in theory, oppose the legalization of abortion have coerced their daughters or partners into undergoing unwanted abortions. Also, many who are against abortion ask themselves, when they see a pregnant homeless woman on the streets, "why do they have so many children?" And although the stigma is disappearing, women who raise their children without a man by their side—be it their choice or circumstance—face mistrust or contempt coming from the same people who wouldn't hesitate to say that "all women want to be mothers." This is a lot more than simple hypocrisy. It's a framework of thinking that detaches motherhood from the intense, irrational, burning desire we experience in our encounters with the world. This narrative states that motherhood is linked with certain rules and conditions: there are circumstances under which it is "desirable" or even "mandatory," and others under which it is criticized, disregarded, and even forbidden. Adrienne Rich put it very plainly: for the paradigm of motherhood as an institution, the most important thing is to keep reproduction under control.

Emilia adopted two little brothers many years ago (today they are both teenagers). They were young, but not babies. Adopting is a lengthy process, but Emilia says it is not actually too long. "Around three or four years," she says, "if you start trying for a baby, a year goes by without anything happening, then you start fertility treatments that last a year or two (maybe more) and you finally get pregnant—the timeline is roughly the same. This is true, of course, if you sign up to adopt children who are two, three, four, five, six years old . . . The older they are, the easier it becomes. And it's also easier if you sign up to adopt more than one, like I did. I said I would accept up to three," she explains. "The problem is that people want a baby, and there are almost no babies in the system . . . So that's when it becomes impossible or very, very difficult." Emilia didn't have many issues. She wanted a family: it didn't matter whether they were babies or not, but she knows that isn't the case for most women. "There are people who have the fantasy of the new-born baby that's fresh and pure, who comes wrapped up in a blanket, but there aren't any of those," she jokes with a hint of a smile. "The children are older and come from very complex situations, in general from having had an awful time although they still can't quite tell you about it. You must be prepared to accept that and to live with it . . . with the guilt of not having been there, even though it's an irrational feeling," she adds, a little more seriously.

In theory, hardly anyone is against adoption but in recent years, as the conceptions of motherhood multiplied, I have a feeling that the narratives surrounding adoption have become invisible, particularly in Argentina. Conversely to what happens in other countries where celebrities frequently adopt children from all over the world, in Argentina, among local celebrities who did not have children in the context of a heterosexual relationship (Marley, Luciana Salazar and Juana Repetto are the first to come to mind), none of them decided to adopt. Rather than judging anyone's personal decisions, it's important to notice what kind of children become social media celebrities, what stories are amplified, and what stories seem to not exist. That fantasy Emilia was talking about, the one of the new-born baby that looks like the protagonist of a diaper advert, didn't come from nowhere: it's a collectively held fantasy fed by a symbolic system in which there are certain kinds of motherhood that are better than others.

But let's face it: feminists never have high expectations of celebrities or religion. We shouldn't be surprised that the emphasis is placed on biology and on a normative and exclusive idea of what "is natural." We can be surprised, however, when these concepts appear in conjunction with feminism. French philosopher and historian Elisabeth Badinter draws attention to what she calls *new naturalism* in her book *The Conflict: How Modern Motherhood Undermines the Status of Women*,[5] published in

English in 2012. The concept refers to a combination of trends that in recent years have become a norm and that point towards reconnecting women with the animal nature that they have been distancing themselves from: avoid caesarean section at all costs, breast-feed on demand, practice co-sleeping (sharing a bed with your baby or child) for a few years, follow attachment parenting (a practice based on various principles, including that of "increasing maternal contact as much as possible" as a key one), returning to fabric diapers, not buying puree or baby food that has been pre-prepared and instead cooking all their food at home. And the list goes on.

To be somewhat fairer than Badinter can sometimes be, I want to clarify that if these are personal decisions, they shouldn't be considered problematic and, furthermore, having the possibility to choose freely whether to follow all these principles should be a given right. I believe that governments should create public policies to allow people (not just women, but all men and women, and all those performing motherhood tasks) to decide how they want to raise their children freely. I also consider many of these ideals to be based on valid arguments and even stem from good intentions: activism in favor of vaginal delivery is linked not only with proving how lucrative the private health system is for performing unnecessary caesarean sections, but also to the obstetric violence that many women experience at such a sensitive and vulnerable moment as childbirth—situations that, until recently, were completely invisible. But I believe there to be a great difference between empowering a woman so that she feels able to ask the obstetrician if the caesarean section is necessary and why, and making her feel—as happened to one of my friends after being brainwashed by societal messages during her pregnancy—that, because she couldn't have a vaginal delivery, her bond with her daughter would be incomplete forever, or that if she doesn't breastfeed—because it hurts her, because she has to go to work, because she has no breastmilk, because she doesn't like it, because she wants to do it but not on demand and not for two years, or because of any other of the infinite possible reasons—she is condemning her baby to a substandard diet that will affect its emotional and intellectual capacity forever. It's one thing making breastfeeding on demand a right that's politically and financially possible to every woman who desires it, and another very different thing turning it into a moral obligation. We should be suspicious of any moral obligations that purport, firstly, that a woman should stay alone at home all day and, secondly, that all the responsibilities of childcare should exclusively fall on her (Badinter states that bottle feeding can be done by the father or anyone who is sharing parenting tasks, breastfeeding cannot).

What interested me the most from Badinter's text is that, from her point of view, this is a narrative that rather than convincing women, is attempting to discourage many of them from venturing into motherhood. From a different starting point, Badinter arrives at Rich's paradox: the way in which institutions extol motherhood does not contribute to the desire and pleasure of the experience, but rather the opposite—it contributes to alienating and convincing many of us who are hesitating, to decide against it. And I include myself in that statement as that is what I felt most identified with.

For Badinter, the belief that motherhood requires "giving one-hundred percent" or not doing it at all not only consipires against the very idea of motherhood but is also more commonly held by women without children than by those who have them: women who have been through the experience, she says, know that deep down it's impossible to be a mother to one-hundred percent of your ability and that you will make mistakes, you will suffer, you will succumb to the temptation of turning on the television to have a moment's peace, or feed them hot dogs on an evening when you're tired. Many of us who aren't mothers (this also appeared in Lina Meruane's argument, with which

I also identify) tend to think that, if we are not willing to give our whole lives to the baby—and in return lose our careers, our sexuality, our social lives, and our public life in general—we shouldn't even try.

Badinter contrasts the archetype of the perfect mother who cooks every night and spends all her free time with her child with the traditionally French outlook on motherhood that she believes to be the secret behind France's highest birth rate in Europe—even higher than places with longer maternity leave periods, such as Scandinavian countries—: the archetype of the mediocre mother. Traditionally in France, explains Badinter, being a mother is one more task among the many in a woman's list. The French woman must continue to have a sexual and social life. She doesn't become a mother and cease to be everything else once she has her first child—no one expects that and, in fact, doing so is frowned upon.

It's hard to say with certainty whether this is truly representative of all French mothers, although Badinter quotes interesting facts (such as French mothers' preference for continuing to work after becoming mothers, for example, and different historical tales about how for centuries French women left their children in the care of other women almost as soon as they were born, and without feeling any guilt). It's unproductive to idealize a system of values that, on surface level, prioritizes the husband's sexual needs—who, as French culture understands, must not be ignored after the arrival of the new-born—over the baby's and the mother's needs. Especially when such a system has historical roots in the near slave labor of nurses and nannies. Despite this, the celebration of mediocrity seems interesting and even reassuring when reconnecting with what Rich calls the experience of motherhood. I don't have to believe that unless I'm willing to be a perfect mother, motherhood isn't for me: I can be a mediocre mother. In any case, as Badinter also illustrates, new naturalism cannot guarantee "perfect children." Although breastfeeding has relative benefits, these (and the disadvantages of formula milk) have been exaggerated by the media—and by social groups that are linked with neo-conservative Christianity[6]—who have promoted statements not backed up by scientific data. The same happens, explains anthropologist Claudia Fonseca, drawing upon John T. Bruer's *The Myth of the First Three Years*,[7] with the idea that the first three years of a person's life determine their intellectual development and even their chances of succeeding in life. There are vague and poorly investigated correlations, but scientifically verified data is far more scarce than what the media and different upbringing manuals have led the public to believe in recent years.

Fonseca, who works in Brazil, places much more emphasis on the classist component of these trends than Badinter—who writes for women belonging to the European middle class. The myth of the first three years that Bruer deconstructs in his book was first used in Brazil to aid a good cause: the justification of programs aimed at children in vulnerable sectors of the population. By August 2018, however, when the Universidad Nacional de San Martín invited Fonseca to visit Argentina—and Bolsonaro's name was not yet recognized by those not living in Brazil—, these theories appeared in the media following a different narrative: children who were born into poverty had not been stimulated enough during the first years of their lives and hence could not have a bright future ahead of them. Their brains, as different journalists explained, would not allow them to become anything other than criminals and a burden for the state. And, of course, the ones to blame were the mothers for choosing to have them without considering this, for consuming illegal substances, and for leading unruly lives that were improper for a mother.

The archetypes that sanctify perfect mothers are far from being harmless because, while they validate certain forms of motherhood, they undermine others: non-biological mothers, women who want or need to work after giving birth, same-sex mothers, mothers who would like to go out dancing, have sex, or engage in activism (notice, for example, the stereotype of the activist mother which circulates in social media today).[8] On the other hand—as Badinter highlights—in a capitalist world, a woman who doesn't earn her own living is not a particularly fortunate one. She's in fact a woman who, if she has to separate from her partner, is left in an extremely complicated situation—not to say completely trapped. We should question the fact that being a woman who is able to stop working is a privilege—assuming she doesn't have an inheritance, own a property, or have a form of income that allows her the luxury of not working, which is extremely rare for women. In fact, it's women from the middle and upper classes who see work as an option and can leave their children in the care of another woman with fewer resources; this is an equation that works only for them. Women with lower incomes, conversely, don't have this option: the kind of work they can do is badly paid, and it isn't financially viable for them to leave their children in the care of someone else (access to daycare and kindergarten in Argentina leaves much to be desired and, even if it was better, it would rarely cover the full working day). This reality became evident in Argentina—if it wasn't already—in March 2017, when the Centro de Implementación de Políticas Públicas para la Equidad y el Crecimiento (CIPPEC) [*Center for the Implementation of Public Policies on Equity and Upbringing*][9] published a case study that questioned the category of young people who neither study nor work (who had been catalogued by other publications as "lazy," "drug addicts," "opportunistic"). The research shows that, out of the 1,080,682 young people in this category, seventy percent were taking care of children, the elderly, or people with disabilities. Unsurprisingly, from that seventy percent, ninety-five percent are young women who look after their children full-time.

In relation to the role of the state, Badinter's book offers an essential learning: to accommodate diverse desires, it is crucial to have a government that is present and that offers an ample variety of public policies. Long maternity leave periods, of course, but also paternity leave—with adequate incentives so that men choose to take them—flexible working so that women can continue performing the tasks of motherhood while they work, government-funded daycare, and kindergartens that cover the working day and are in diverse locations, ideally in the areas where women usually work and study. The state cannot say that the only option when looking after your own children is to stay at home if all it offers is inadequate maternity leave, says Badinter, though in a way, that's the message it's communicating. Would this change with a reform? Would childcare and related tasks be distributed more equally between men and women? We assume that they would, but we don't know to what extent. To which point would state regulations modify behavioral patterns that are in general only exposed in private? This continues to be an unanswered question, but what is certain is that no law can make anyone change a diaper. However, a state that supports female independence not only offers women other tools to advocate for a fair distribution of household tasks, but also modifies the incentives system and changes the prevailing narrative.

Relationships between women that are based on solidarity are also essential. In the face of a precarious political and financial system on which we place demands knowing that the best possible outcome is to receive a fifteen-day paternity leave (instead of the current one on offer in Argentina which is two days long and therefore a temporary solution) we must organize to prevent childcare from becoming not only an increasingly demanding task, but also an increasingly solitary one.

Personally, after spending many months reading debates between mothers on the internet, reading books on the subject as if I was undercover, and having conversations with women who had and women who didn't have children, I'm left with something new yet inconclusive: if we struggle to talk about motherhood like we struggle to talk about sex, it's not only because of the stigma and preconceptions around them. If both struggles are intricately related to language it's because both motherhood and sex are profoundly linked with desire (or the lack of it) as the history of philosophy explains, not to mention Derrida. Language has a universal vocation, it demands that we use the word "motherhood" to talk about your motherhood and mine, even though they are completely different. It demands rules and generalizations when there is nothing less generic or less regulated that the shape of our desire. Thinking about desire demands the contrary instead: a morality that is specific rather than all-encompassing, a morality based on specifics and not generalizations. It's an authentically philosophical challenge to detach oneself from this hunger for universality and approach the other's experience without attempting to identify it with one's own. That difficulty can often be the foundation of the failed yet well-meaning attempts of many women to understand each other. Mediocre mothers and naturalist mothers; women who have children and women who don't, all try to understand each other and the categories they fall under. And that, which can be implemented in the intellectual sphere, when combined with physicality, generates new situations. Learning how to observe and how to love diversity without reducing it to a never-ending generalization is the key to everything.

# EPILOGUE
## STARTING OVER

Writing this book was a lot more painful than I thought it would be. When I started it, I had already been writing journalistic articles on how my generation managed or pretended to manage emotional and sexual relationships. I thought this would be a similar experience, but it wasn't. The immersion required for my notes, which took ten days of reading and resulted in two or three pages per article, allowed me to skim through each topic without delving into the parts that hurt me most. This process was different.

I chose "The Final Question" as the title for the last chapter, though only now do I realize that it is because the other chapters are also that, questions, and that they are all just as inconclusive as the consideration of whether I am going to become a mother or not. I don't know what kind of relationship suits me best—if it's a monogamous one, an open one, a stable or a fleeting one. I don't know how to navigate the contradiction between desire for novelty and desire for warmth. I don't know how to continue to offer myself now that I don't want to ever lose myself again. I do what I can, and I can do very little. I don't have advice or solutions. I only have tentative ideas, readings, and intuitions. I also have one certainty that I struggle to illustrate in a single sentence: it's related to the transient nature of answers and the inherent impossibility of truly grasping any of this. The lessons learned in one relationship are rarely useful in another one: we have an incredible talent for making new mistakes every time.

Even so, I'm not a pessimist. I believe in the value of experience, in the reality of it; and in that sense, I do consider myself to have grown, and that all of us—men and women—are growing collectively. Different generations go through their own crossroads: we all are or were "the transitional generation," of a given transition. Our generation experienced many—in the spheres of the emotional, professional, financial, political—but, if I had to summarize them in one single dilemma, I would say that our transition was that of the tension between opposing forces. On one extreme we have the old traditions of communal life: the traditional family, nationalism, belonging to a certain culture, and sharing a language. On the other extreme, what is presented as an alternative is a kind of neutral individualism: consumerism, competition, and caring and protecting oneself. Traditional conservatism insists—increasingly violently—that we follow the first extreme as the only recipe for happiness. Those who do not marry and have children will remain alone, those who fight with their people (people who are randomly assigned to you at birth or by the culture you were born in) will relinquish the possibility of ever feeling at home. We are told that outside of these structures, all that's left is desolation. A new type of conservatism suggests that the other extreme is an available option. Empowerment is working, earning money, having sex, consuming. Relationships, under this new paradigm, are also thought of as objects of consumption: if it makes me feel good, I'll keep it; if it takes up too much room, I'll discard it.

I'm not writing this from a place of moral superiority but from the treadmill at the gym, where a Trap singer is defending her independence by singing at the top of her lungs that she doesn't need a man to support her because she has her own money. Aside from poetry, her lyrics are filled with irony, and I recognize myself in this misunderstanding. I argued with my community and most of my family during my adolescence; I justified my ability to insert myself in the market—without thinking, until I reached a certain age, about the privilege and alienation this entailed—as a way of not needing anything or anyone. I still have enough energy to run while I listen to these songs about buying an expensive car or checking the time on a Rolex, though now I listen to them from a different perspective.

I believe that what feminists are trying to do is invent a third option: an ethical otherness that is not equivalent to the ethics of sacrifice; the idea that happiness can be collective without being oppressive. Sorority consists of much more than a theoretical solidarity between female identities. It consists of thinking of your chosen community, of relationships that are based on the possibility of sharing rather than negotiating. There is a model that we can follow, and that model is friendship: a relationship that is chosen but that, once chosen, also comes with obligations and leaves us vulnerable in the face of others.

Friendships exist in the margins of Orthodox Judaism, on the edge of what isn't said, isn't named and doesn't matter. The fundamental ties are biological and communal, ties with the people who belong to the "right" group. There's no reason why you would help someone who isn't part of your family, particularly if they're not Jewish. Nor is there any reason why you would expect someone to help you. In that sense, to me the secular world meant seeing the possibility of friendship. I have blind faith in friendship. I believe that friendship, understood both in a personal and political way, can transform everything though we don't yet know how. It's a model, something to always keep in mind. Queer communities know this: they experience community in a liberating way.

I do not know what the future holds; I even struggle to unravel the present. But, for now, following in Judith Butler's footsteps, what I propose is resistance: choosing between inherited structures and a wild individualism, and accepting that those are our only options. It's an uncomfortable, marginal—in the most literal sense of the word—position. Anyone who has ever tried to question the relationships within their community or family knows it: daring to fight for your own desires, despite what we've been taught, pushes you to the margins as if you had been wiped off the map—particularly if you don't embrace the doctrines of the market and the industry of a "business-minded" empowerment. In the margins of these pages, there is room for everything to be written. It's understandable that we're afraid. Even so, we are going to build communities in which our emotions can exist freely. We are going to take advantage of marginality to look at oppression closely; to look at the inherited oppressive forces that are being marketed as a novelty. We are going to defend our desire but also the dynamics of care by demanding public policies that allow us to organize our relationships without thinking of who will support us when we need help. We aim to foster the material conditions where our approach to others isn't rooted in competition. We are going to create the symbolic conditions that will allow us to name what hurts us and stop it before it's too late, and before the only question that remains to be answered is what the punishment will be.

We are going to try.

# NOTES

## PREFACE

[1] Federici, Silvia (2021): *Caliban and the Witch: Women, the Body and Primitive Accumulation*, Penguin Classics.

## CHAPTER 1

[1] I will discuss this concept at length in Chapter 7.

[2] Coontz, Stephanie (2005): *Marriage, a History: How Love Conquered Marriage*, Penguin Random House.

[3] Arranged marriages (not the same as forced marriages as in an arranged marriage there is usually some form of consent between both parties) are still relatively common in India and in the most orthodox sectors of Jewish and Muslim communities, just to mention some well-known examples.

[4] A good reference for the conceptual relation between Modernism and romantic love is *Why Love Hurts* by Eva Illouz, Cambridge, Polity Press (2012).

[5] Kottman, Paul A. (2012): "Defying the Stars: Tragic Love and the Struggle for Freedom in Romeo and Juliet," *Shakespeare Quarterly*, vol. 63, no. 1, Spring, pp. 1-38.

[6] De Beauvoir, Simone (1959): "Brigitte Bardot and the Lolita Syndrome," *Esquire*, 1st August; available online: https://classic.esquire.com/article/1959/8/1/brigitte-bardot-and-the-lolita-syndrome

[7] MPDG is a stock character in pop culture. Film critic Nathan Rabin, who coined the term after watching Kristen Dunst in *Elizabethtown* (2005), describes her as someone who "exists solely in the fevered imaginations of sensitive writer-directors to teach broodingly soulful young men to embrace life and its infinite mysteries and adventures." These are characters that are supposedly chic and loveable but do not really have a personality or any true interests of their own. They exist solely to satisfy the male protagonist (and the male spectator), and to teach them to enjoy life and follow their dreams and aspirations. See also: Rabin, Nathan (2007): "The Bataan Death March of Whimsy Case File #1: Elizabethtown," *AV Club*, 25th January; available online: https://www.av-club.com/the-bataan-death-march-of-whimsy-case-file-1-elizabet-1798210595

[8] To support these intuitions (and learn about the landscape of women's magazines in Argentina during the past decades) I had a very useful conver-

sation with Uruguayan historian Isabella Cosse, researcher at CONICET and local specialist in the history of the family.

[9] Cosse, Isabella: "*Claudia*: la revista de la mujer moderna en la Argentina de los años sesenta (1957-1973)," *Mora*, vol. 17, no. 1; available online: http://www.scielo.org.ar/scielo.php?script=sci_arttext&pid=S1853-001X2011000100007

[10] Translator's note: Gilda was an Argentine cumbia singer and songwriter of such importance that, after her death in 1996, she began to be regarded as a saint for Argentinians. The original titles of the songs mentioned and quoted above are "No me arrepiento de este amor" and "Corazón valiente."

## CHAPTER 2

[1] Wiener, Gabriela (2018): "El sexo de las supervivientes," *El País* (online version), 30th April; available online: www.eldiario.es/zonacritica/sexosuper-vivientes_6_766483345.html

[2] The number of single-occupant homes has been growing all over the world since the eighties, and Argentina is no exception. According to official statistics, only 10.4% were single-occupant homes; thirty years later, the 2010 census claimed that 17.7% of households in Argentina housed only one person. In the city of Buenos Aires, the change was even more abrupt, although in 1980 the percentage was already higher than the national figure at 15.9%, in 2015 this increased to 35.6% of single-occupant homes. Source: INDEC [National Institute of Statistics and Census of Argentina] and Dirección General de Estadística y Censos de la Ciudad de Buenos Aires [General Centre of Statistics and Census of the City of Buenos Aires].

[3] Instituto Nacional de Estadística de España (INE) [National institute of Statistics of Spain].

[4] Friedan, Betty (1964): *The Feminine Mystique*, revised edition, Penguin Classics (2010).

[5] Álvarez, Silvina (2012): "The personal autonomy of women. An approximation to relational autonomy and the construction of options," published and presented at the seminary of the School of Law of Universidad de Palermo; available online: https://www.palermo.edu/derecho/pdf/La-autonomia-de-las-mujeres.pdf

[6] Philosopher Heather Widdows explains how aspirations work in relation to social class. Although she examines the issue of beauty standards, her hypothesis can be applied to emotional ideals. An ideal can demand a lot of resources in order to be satisfied (having a body that is perfect according to hegemonic standards, for example, requires—aside from certain genetic traits—time and money, and the same happens with the "perfect couple" in relation to what I have been discussing here), but those who cannot access these resources are also affected by these ideals: they will try to adhere to them as best as their possibilities allow, and they will suffer because that is not enough. Widdows, Heather (2018): *Perfect Me: Beauty as an Ethical Ideal*, Princeton, Princeton University Press.

[7] Illouz, Eva (2007): *Cold Intimacies: The Making of Emotional Capitalism*, Polity Press.

[8] Szalai, Jennifer (2015): "The Complicated Origins of 'Having It All,'" *The New York Times Magazine*, 2nd January; available online: www.nytimes.com/2015/01/04/magazine/the-complicated-origins-of-having-it-all.html

[9] Boeing, Niels and Lebert, Andreas (2015): "Byung-Chul Han: 'I am Sorry, but those Are Facts,'" *SkorpionUK* blog, 3rd November, available online: https://skorpionuk.wordpress.com/2015/11/03/byung-chul-han-im-sorry-but-those-are-facts/

[10] An article in *The Washington Post* gathered the best available data on the asymmetry of what are known as trailing spouses (people who relocate for their partners' jobs), which tend to be mostly women. ElBoghdady, Dina (2014): "Why Couples Move for a Man's Job, but not a Woman's," *The Washington Post*, 28th November; available online: www.washingtonpost.com/news/wonk/wp/2014/11/28/why-couples-move-for-a-mans-jobbut-not-a-womans/?utm_term=.e19b9428ac14

## CHAPTER 3

[1] Anapol, Deborah (2012): *Polyamory in the 21st Century: Love and Intimacy with Multiple Partners*, Lanham, Rowman & Littlefield Publishers.

[2] Cosse, Isabella (2010): *Pareja, sexualidad y familia en los años sesenta*, Buenos Aires, Siglo XI.

[3] Lerner, Gerda (22 Oct. 1987): *The Creation of Patriarchy*, Oxford University Press, USA; Revised Edition.

[4] The question of whether monogamy is "natural" or not for humans poses many conceptual problems. Biology rarely speaks of what is straightforwardly "natural" and, from a logical point of view, this is a fallacious deduction as there is no correlation between what is "natural" and what is "right." In any case, biology has explored the link between sexual conduct and evolution (if human beings evolve or not to become monogamous, for example, or what sexual conducts could be genetically related to make it easier or harder). Biologist David P. Barash and psychologist Judith Eve Lipton researched this subject for many years: in their first co-authored book *Myth Of Monogamy: Fidelity and Infidelity in Animals and People* (Griffin; reprint edition, May 2002), they gathered evidence that demonstrated that strict monogamy is a highly improbable and difficult conduct for human beings due to evolutionary reasons (which also broke the prejudice that monogamy is in fact "natural and easy" for women). However, years later, in *Strange Bedfellows: The Surprising Connection Between Sex, Evolution and Monogamy* (Bellevue Literary Press, 2009, New York), they explored another pool of evidence that pointed in the opposite direction by examining the evolutionary advantages of monogamy. Nature, though many conservative people disagree, has no intention of giving us definitive answers about how to run our relationships.

[5] Federici, Silvia (July 2021): *Caliban and the Witch*.

[6] This is expertly explained in the chapter "Why Women Are Paid Less" of the documental series *Explained*, co-produced by news outlet Vox and Netflix. In countries that have made great advances in decreasing explicit professional

discrimination against women, the disparity in care work is the main responsible factor contributing to the persisting gender pay gap (by having less freedom to stay in the office late and gain "merit" that will result in a promotion).

[7] This detail is taken from the feminist economist Mercedes D'Alessandro in the debate "The agenda of equality" organized by the Laboratorio de Políticas Públicas y el Centro de Estudios Municipales y Provinciales (CE-MUPRO), [Laboratory of Public Policy and Centre of Municipal and Provincial Studies], available online: https://www.mercedesdalessandro.com/noesamor

[8] Despentes, Virginie (translated by Frank Wynne, 2021): *King Kong Theory*, FSG Originals.

[9] When feminist journalist Marta Dillon said that "the heterosexual relationship is a risk factor," she was referring to this. She was ridiculed and accused of being a "feminazi" because, of course, talking about the streets being a dangerous place is reassuring, but revealing that our homes and families are even more dangerous is an incredibly discomforting message. Marziotta, Gisela (2018): "Marta Dillon: 'La pareja heterosexual es un factor de riesgo para la vida de las mujeres,'" *Infobae*, 3rd June, available online: www.infobae.com/sociedad/2018/06/03/marta-dillon-la-pareja-heterosexual-es-un-factorde-riesgo-para-la-vida-de-las-mujeres

[10] "El perfil de los hogares de la Ciudad en 2015" [The Outline of Homes in the City in 2015], report published by the Dirección General de Estadística y Censos de la Ciudad de Buenos Aires [General Centre of Statistics and Census of the City of Buenos Aires], available online: www.estadisticaciudad.gob.ar/eyc/?p=62000

[11] This difference could partly be linked to women having a longer life expectancy than men; however, according to demographers Mabel Ariño and Victoria Mazzeo, it's also linked with the functioning of the marriage market. From 1980 to 2008, significantly more men remarried (after a divorce) than women, due to demographic reasons but also clearly general ones. "Aside from the distinct individual behavior between men and women when it comes to remarrying," the authors write, "the differences between gender in the marriage market (more women than men) form an intervening variable. The end of married life often leaves women with fewer chances to form a new relationship. Apart from being at an age that might be less favorable in the marital market, they are also burdened by the marks left by that breakup, especially if they have to take on the maternal role and household responsibilities. See also: Ariño, Mabel y Mazzeo, Victoria (2009): "Siglo XXI en la Ciudad de Buenos Aires: ¿cómo armar pareja y cómo vivir en familia?," report presented at the X Jornadas Argentinas de Estudios de Población Argentina, San Fernando del Valle de Catamarca, Asociación de Estudios de Población de la Argentina; available online: www.aacademica.org/000-058/24.pdf

[12] Baigorria, Osvaldo (edited by), (2006): *El amor libre. Eros y anarquía* [*Free Love. Eros and Anarchy*], de Anarres, Buenos Aires.

[13] Ibid., p. 9.

[14] Ibid., p. 10.

[15] Recently, some feminists have been referencing the works of Andrea Dworkin and other radical feminists to advocate for a biologically deterministic and exclusive understanding of what it means to "be a woman." I want to highlight that, specifically regarding Dworkin, such an interpretation of her writings is biased. In fact, in her book *Woman Hating*, she clearly writes that "every transsexual has the right to survival on his/her own terms. That means every transsexual is entitled to a sex-change operation, and it should be provided by the community as one of its functions." (Dworkin, Andrea [1974]: *Woman Hating*, E. P. Dutton, New York, p. 186).

[16] Dworkin, Andrea (1983): *Right-Wing Women*, Coward, McCann & Geoghegan, New York.

[17] The word "heterosexual" refers to sexual and emotional preferences. The word "cisgender," instead, refers to gender identity. A cis person is one who identifies with the gender they were assigned to at birth; on the contrary, a trans person does not identify with the gender they were assigned to at birth (they can identify with another gender, none, as gender fluid, as non-binary, etc.).

[18] Frankfurt, Harry (2004): *The Reasons of Love*, Princeton University Press.

[19] Lorey, Isabell (2015): *State of Insecurity. Government of the Precarious*, Verso Books; Reprint edition. P. 16.

[20] Ibid., p 23.

[21] Ibid., p 43.

[22] Mononormative describes the idea that any sexual and emotional agreement that falls outside of monogamy is less valuable, that monogamy is not an option among many but the best or even the only option.

[23] hooks, bell (1990): "Marginality as Site of Resistance," in *Out There: Marginalization and Contemporary Culture*, edited by Russell Ferguson, Martha Gever, Trinh T. Minh-ha, and Cornel West, New York, MIT Press.

CHAPTER 4

[1] The issue of single Orthodox women and their "eternally young" or "social pariahs" status was discussed in the North American Jewish blogging sphere in 2017 after Emily Shire's article (2017): "In Orthodox Jewish Circles, Single Women Are Largely Forgotten," *The Washington Post*, 5th January; available online: www.washingtonpost.com/news/soloish/wp/2017/01/05/in-orthodox-jewish-circlessingle-women-are-largely-forgotten/?utm_term=.de8e3d824e5c

[2] The story of these New Yorkers can be found in Velsey, Kim (2016): "An Upper West Side Share where Roommates Are the Selling Point," *The New York Times*, 23rd December; available online: www.nytimes.com/2016/12/23/realestate/an-upper-west-side-share-whereroommates-are-the-selling-point.html

[3] Witt, Emily (2016): *Future Sex*, FSG Press, New York.

[4] Illouz, Eva (2012): *Why Love Hurts*.

[5] Flynn, Gillian (2012): "The Cool Girl Monologue," in *Gone Girl*; available online: https://genius.com/Gillian-flynn-gone-girl-cool-girl-monologue-book-annotated

[6] Illouz, Eva (2012): *Why Love Hurts*. When the author says that the process has become "more subjective and individualistic," she refers to the way in which choosing a partner begins to be an individual's responsibility and no longer their family or clan's. Today, each person chooses their partner according to their own standards and desires (as happens in a trade transaction). What Illouz endeavors to highlight is the extent to which those standards and desires are conditioned by social structures and power dynamics.

[7] Sorority refers to the solidarity between women and the need to support another woman even when our initial intuition is to mistrust her (it also implies the acceptance that the patriarchy imposed on us an untrustworthy and competitive impulse); the word comes from *soror*, which in Latin means "sister."

[8] Illouz, Eva (2012): *Why Love Hurts*.

[9] See, among other examples, "Children Aren't Key to Women's Happiness: Study," 8th May 2007; available online: https://www.reuters.com/article/%20us-mothers-happiness/children-arent-key-towomenshappiness-study-idUSL0810277020070508

[10] Bruch, Elizabeth E. and Newman, Mark E. J. (2018): "Aspirational Pursuit of Mates in Online Dating Markets," *Science Advances*, vol. 4, n° 8, August; available online: https://www.science.org/doi/10.1126/sciadv.aap9815

[11] As Illouz says, "research shows that men benefit more from marriage than women do. Given that, in most marriages, women tend to serve the man, this is hardly surprising. Moreover, women not only serve their husbands, they encourage their 'kin-keeping': that is, they keep intact men's relationships to their children and to other family members. Finally, marriage provides the incentive for men to earn more and remain healthy." In Illouz, Eva (2012): *Why Love Hurts*.

[12] Weigel, Mora (2016): *Labor of Love: The Invention of Dating*, Farrar, Straus and Giroux.

[13] Greif, Geoffrey L. (2008): *Buddy System: Understanding Male Friendships*, Oxford University Press.

[14] Manne, Kate (2017): *Down Girl: The Logic of Misogyny*, Oxford University Press.

## CHAPTER 5

[1] Grindr, for example, one of the most popular apps within the male gay community, works in a different way: anyone can speak and send pictures to anyone, something that Tinder and Happn do not allow (probably to avoid women leaving the app after receiving dick pics).

[2] Each app has its own term for "likes." I use "like" as a generic term for all because I see it being used in an informal manner.

[3] Witt, Emily, *Future Sex*.

[4] These were two chat services that were extremely popular in the early two-thousands. They were not chatrooms like Terra, for example, where you crossed paths with people you didn't know. They were more similar to mes-

saging services such as Facebook Messenger; to add a new contact you had to exchange certain details (email in the case of MSN or a long number that for us was our second ID in the case of ICQ).

[5] These groups were a kind of combination of a forum and an email list where people could share information and debate topics that they were interested in.

[6] Turkle, Sherry (2015): *Reclaiming Conversation. The Power of Talk in a Digital Age*, New York, Penguin Press, p. 7.

[7] By "early days of the internet," I approximately refer to the first decade of the third millennium. In 2007, Facebook and Twitter became global corporations, and the first model of iPhone was launched. Journalist Thomas Friedman writes that 2007 was the pivotal year of the age of information in *Thank You for Being Late: An Optimist's Guide to Thriving in the Age of Accelerations* (Farrar, Straus and Giroux, 2016). In Argentina, however, the massification of networks and smartphones was somewhat slower (the newspaper *La Nación*, for example, opened its Twitter account in 2009), and so I prefer a hazier approach to the differences between the first and the second decade of 2000 rather than selecting a specific year.

[8] The data about smartphones is sourced from consultancy firm Deloitte; the comparison with bank accounts comes from a study ran by the company Sos Móvil and was corroborated against data from the World Bank, shared by CEO Raúl Zarif in Sticco, Daniel (2017): "In Argentina, there are more than three users of smartphones for each person who has a bank account." *Infobae*, 13th March, available online: https://www.infobae.com/economia/2017/03/13/en-la-argentina-hay-mas-de-3-usuarios-de-celulares-por-cada-uno-con-cuenta-bancaria/

[9] She explicitly discussed this, for example, in Penny, Laurie y Weigel, Moira (2016): "Is Love Necessary? Laurie Penny in Conversation with Moira Weigel," *New Statesman*, 31st May; available online: https://www.newstatesman.com/politics/2016/05/love-necessary-laurie-penny-conversation-moira-weigel

[10] The author expands on this point in Federici, Silvia (August 1, 2020): *Revolution at Point Zero: Housework, Reproduction, and Feminist Struggle*, PM Press; Second edition.

[11] Haywood, Chris (2018): *Men, Masculinity and Contemporary Dating*, Basingstoke, Palgrave Macmillan.

[12] Ibid.

[13] Manne, Kate (2017): *Down Girl: The Logic of Misogyny*.

[14] Schilling, Dave (2018): "Why Do We Think Only Men Ghost," *MEL Magazine*; available online: https://melmagazine.com/en-us/story/why-do-we-think-only-men-ghost

[15] Haywood, Chris, (2018): *Men, Masculinity and Contemporary Dating*.

[16] Levinas, Emmanuel (1985): *Ethics and Infinity: Conversations with Philippe Nemo*, Duquesne University Press.

[17] I know that for most women Aziz Ansari is cancelled—that is to say, he has been declared a *persona non grata*—but I speak of cancelled individuals in the last chapter, so I will deal with this issue later in the book.

[18] Ansari, Aziz y Klinenberg, Eric (2015): *Modern Romance: An Investigation*, New York, Penguin.

[19] According to a study by *MIT Technology Review* published in October 2017 (https://www.technologyreview.com/2017/10/10/148701/first-evidence-that-online-dating-is-changing-the-nature-of-society/), online dating is the second most used way of meeting heterosexual partners and the first one when meeting same-sex partners.

CHAPTER 6

[1] Hess, Amanda (2018): "'I Feel Pretty' and the Rise of Beauty-Standard Denialism," *The New York Times* (online edition), 23rd April; available online: www.nytimes.com/2018/04/23/movies/i-feel-pretty-amy-schumer-beauty.html

[2] The number of deaths associated to Anorexia Nervosa quoted by Wolf have been criticized as exaggerated or unfounded.

[3] Wolf, Naomi (2002): *The Beauty Myth. How Images of Beauty Are Used Against Women*, New York, Harper Collins.

[4] I remember perfectly the chapter in *Little Women* titled "Meg Goes to Vanity Fair" in which Meg goes to a party with her wealthy friends and dresses up to look like them. When her mother finds out, she explains to them that all of that is worthless, that what matters is what is inside, and that preoccupying oneself with looking pretty is beneath them. Aside from the puritan subtext (Meg is reprimanded for dressing up but also for flirting), I remember reading this when I was eleven or twelve years old and feeling shocked at the idea that someone could tell you off for wanting to look pretty, instead of encouraging and applauding you. Not even in my Orthodox world it would have occurred to me that beauty and "personal care" could be anything other than positive.

[5] Widdows, Heather (2018): *Perfect Me: Beauty as an Ethical Ideal*, Princeton University Press.

[6] Contrera, Laura and Cuello, Nicolás (2016): "Neoliberalismo magro" ["Lean Neoliberalism"], *Página/12*, 17th January; available online: https://www.pagina12.com.ar/diario/elpais/1-290493-2016-01-17.html

[7] Pinhas, Leora and others (2008): "Disordered Eating in Jewish Adolescent Girls," *Canadian Journal of Psychiatry*, vol. 53, no. 9, September; available online: www.ncbi.nlm.nih.gov/pubmed/18801223

[8] These initials stand for Mom I'd Like to Fuck and refer to fantasizing about "older" women, who in practice could be anything from thirty-five to sixty years old. MILF is used as a category in porn sites to find videos with women within that age range. In 2017, it was the term with most searches by men in *Pornhub*, the third largest porn site in the world, according to an article by Rense, Sarah (2018): "The Human Race Really Outdid Itself with Porn Searches in 2018," *Esquire*, 12th December; available online: www.esquire.com/lifestyle/sex/news/a52061/most-popular-porn-searches

CHAPTER 7

[1] Segato, Rita (2003): "Las estructuras elementales de la violencia. Ensayos sobre género entre la antropología, el psicoanálisis y los derechos humanos" ["The Elemental Structures of Violence. Essays on Gender, Anthropology, Psychoanalysis, and Human Rights"], Bernal, Universidad Nacional de Quilmes.

[2] Abdulali, Sohaila (2018): *What We Talk About When We Talk About Rape*, New York, The New Press.

[3] The concept of rape culture was developed by second generation feminists during the decade of the seventies. Most likely—though there are other versions—it was first written about in 1974, in the book *Rape: The First Sourcebook for Women* edited by Noreen Connell and Cassandra Wilson as a tool for militancy to be used by the New York Radical Feminists. The idea that rape and violence against women are not exceptional or rare occurrences but endemic of our social fabric (and that, for that reason, the only way to eradicate them is the feminist revolution) appears for the first time from within this group of feminists.

[4] Lorde, Audre (2007): *Sister Outsider*, New York, Penguin Random House.

[5] Derrida, Jacques (1992): *Deconstruction and the Possibility of Justice*, New York, Routledge.

[6] Ramón, María del Mar (2018): "Coger sin querer y sin decir que no (una historia sobre consentimiento)" ["Fucking without wanting to and without saying no (a story of consent)"], *Nómada*, 26th October.

[7] Sobrino, Belén (2018): *Breaking the mould: changing belief systems and gender norms to eliminate violence against women*, Oxford, Oxfam, July; available online: https://oxfamilibrary.openrepository.com/bitstream/handle/10546/620524/rr-breaking-the-mould-250718-summ-en.pdf

[8] Quote in Segato, Rita (2003): "Las estructuras elementales de la violencia."

[9] Ibid.

[10] Scully, Diana (1994): *Understanding Sexual Violence: A Study of Convicted Rapists*, New York and London, Routledge.

[11] This prejudice, on the other hand, is characteristic of heterosexuality and stems from a fear of speaking openly about sex: it is clear on Grindr, the most popular dating app used by the male gay community, where profiles already clarify whether they will perform oral sex or not, whether they want you to come to their house or would rather go to yours, whether they prefer the active or the passive role, or if they are versatile, etc. Nobody there seems to believe that explicit language can "kill desire."

[12] Translator's note: relating to Carlos Saúl Menem, who served as president of Argentina from 1989 to 1999.

[13] Sociologist Eleonor Faur explores this in a similar way in her column: Faur, Eleonor (2018): "La acción de las actrices argentinas se aleja del escrache para constituir una estrategia política," [The Action of Argentine Actors Moves Away from Public Shaming to Build a Political Strategy], *Perfil*, 16th December; available online: https://www.perfil.com/noticias/elobservador/la-desnudez-del-emperador.phtml?

[14] One of the most detailed considerations on this concept can be found in *Ask: Building Consent Culture*, a collection of texts edited by queer writer Kitty Stryker, with a prologue by essayist Laurie Penny. The book points at the subject from different angles: the way in which we struggle to think of consent in different relationships, the educational strategies used to discuss consent with teenagers, and the difficulty we have in thinking about sexual violence from a standpoint that is not punishment, among others.

[15] Some theories have begun to explore the connection between late capitalism, precarization, and the way in which the removal of the government posits that labor and emotional relationships become increasingly mutually ambiguous. Essayist Remedios Zafra, for example, examines this in *El entusiasmo. Precariedad y trabajo creativo en la era digital* [ *Enthusiasm. Precarity and Creative Labour in the Digital Age*], (Barcelona, Anagrama, 2018); artist and writer Martha Rosler, in a brilliant text titled "Why Are People Being so Nice?," *e-flux*, no. 77, November 2016; available online: https://www.e-flux.com/journal/77/76185/why-are-people-being-so-nice/.

## CHAPTER 8

[1] Meruane, Lina (2018): *Contra los hijos* [*Against Children*], Buenos Aires, Random House.

[2] Rich, Adrienne (1986): *Of Woman Born. Motherhood as Experience and Institution*, New York, Norton and Company, p. 47.

[3] Ibid. p. 49.

[4] There is an interesting paradox in this distribution: raising children, in the Orthodox world, is a female task but it is distributed among different people instead of falling on one woman, as is the case in most families in the secular world today. I have also never heard an Orthodox woman say that a bottle was the enemy or say that she felt guilty for having to leave her babies with another person: they have so many children to look after simultaneously that they would not even entertain the idea of "living for your baby."

[5] Badinter, Elisabeth (2012): *The Conflict: How Modern Motherhood Undermines the Status of Women*, New York, Metropolitan Books.

[6] La Leche League (an international non-profit organization that promotes breastfeeding across the world), explains Badinter, has always been linked with Christian movements that advocated for women to return to their homes.

[7] In *The Myth of the First Three Years: A New Understanding of Early Brain Development and Lifelong Learning* (New York, Free Press, 2002), John Bruer explores the available evidence in favor of the hypothesis that the first three years of a child's life are decisive for its cerebral development and, in general terms, reaches the conclusion that there is not sufficient information to corroborate this.

[8] This stereotype circulates on social media throughout Latin America. Initially, the phrase was used by young mothers, often housewives, who defended their desire to be mothers alongside their desire to have fun. Later, the

phrase took a different angle and began to be used by those who criticized these women with racist, classist, and chauvinistic insults. As explained in the article written by Paz Frontera, Agustina (2018): "Mamás luchonas" ["Fighting Mothers"], *Latfem*, 14th November; available online: https://www.latfem.org/mamas-luchonas

[9] This case study is available online: https://www.cippec.org/textual/los-mal-llamados-jovenes-nini-son-chicos-y-chicas-que-no-estudian-porque-cuidan-67-el-95-son-mujeres/

## About the Author

Tamara Tenenbaum was born in Buenos Aires, Argentina, in 1989. She is a lecturer at the Universidad de Buenos Aires and teaches Creative Writing at the Universidad Nacional de las Artes, Argentina. She writes for *Vice*, *La Nación*, *Infobae*, *Anfibia*, and *Orsai*. In 2017 she published a collection of poems and in 2018 she was awarded the Premio Ficciones for her book *Nadie vive tan cerca de nadie*. Her first long-form essay, *The End of Love*, has been published to great critical acclaim in Latin America, Spain, and Italy.